D1348972

AN ILLUSTRATED GUIDE TO
WORLD WAR II
TANKS
AND FIGHTING VEHICLES

a Salamander book

Published by Salamander Books Limited
LONDON

AN ILLUSTRATED GUIDE TO
WORLD WAR II
TANKS
AND FIGHTING VEHICLES

A Salamander Book

© 1981 Salamander Books Ltd,
Salamander House,
27 Old Gloucester Street,
London WC1N 3AF,
United Kingdom.

ISBN 0 86101 083 3

Distributed in the United Kingdom by
New English Library Ltd.

Contents

Tanks are arranged chronologically within national groups

Credits

Editorial consultant:
Christopher F. Foss, author of and
contributor to many technical
reference books concerned with
armored fighting vehicles.

Editor: Ray Bonds
Designer: Lloyd Martin

Colour drawings:
© Salamander Books Ltd., and
© Profile Publications Ltd.
Photographs: The publishers wish
to thank all the official international
governmental archives, weapons
systems manufacturers and private
collections who have supplied
photographs for this book.

Printed: in Belgium by
Henri Proost et Cie.

INTRODUCTION

When tanks first appeared on the battlefield during World War I their primary role was that of supporting the infantry and often the gains achieved by the tanks were lost as insufficient infantry could be brought up to consolidate the advances made. Between the wars, tank development continued on varying scales in many countries but tactics (and therefore specifications and designs) tended to be rooted generally in the World War I concept. A notable exception, of course, were the German designers and visionary commanders, such as Guderian. Germany began to re-arm in the early 1930s and her Panzer divisions struck terror throughout Western Europe. The Blitzkrieg tactics were the result of uniting infiltration tactics with the tank and substituting dive-bombers for slow-moving artillery. In particular, the spearhead of the German attack on France in May 1940 was the eight out of ten specially trained Panzer divisions.

World War II became the war of mechanisation, and the the tank the symbol of mobile warfare. The Germans used tanks en masse and in conjunction with infantry, artillery, engineers and air power. But the Blitzkrieg could only really work against poorly trained and badly led troops whose morale was at a low ebb, so that when Panzers came

up against determined and disciplined resistance they could be contained and mauled by artillery and Allied tanks.

Though they played a relatively insignificant part in World War II, light tanks were the most numerous types in service at the start. The tank was proved to be a decisive battlefield weapon, but the war saw a natural and inevitable growth in counterweapons. As anti-tank capability increased, so did the adoption of heavier armour and size and weight of tanks – to ridiculous proportions in some cases (the German Maus and Elefant, for example).

Standardisation and reliability were also of fundamental importance in tank warfare – the Americans fought almost the entire war with just two basic models. The Allies learned to build tanks with thicker and better armour and more powerful guns, and how to use guns with more effect, so that the Panzers, while remaining formidable, ceased to be unbeatable.

Nor could the Germans hope to match the tank production capabilities of the Allies, and the real strength of the Alliance lay in the American genius for realising technological ideals in terms of engineering, and then mass-producing the result: by the end of the war, the USA, Britain and Russia had built 200,000 tanks.

FRANCE

During World War I France built three tanks in quantity: the two-man Renault FT-17 (over 4,000) and the Saint Chamond and Schneider assault tanks (400 of each). In 1920, though tank development did continue both for the cavalry and the infantry, tanks were assigned to the infantry as they were in other countries. The French continued to see land warfare in terms of long lines of forces spread out along a front, instead of in powerful and mobile concentrations on narrow fronts: and it was forces such as the latter which were to defeat the over-stretched French defences some 20 years later.

By May 1940 the French Army had some 2,800 light tanks (R-35/R-40, H-35/H-39 and FCM-36), 384 B1 and B1-bis heavy tanks, 416 S-35 mediums, 864 cavalry tanks and some 2,000 modernised FT-17s. Many of these tanks were superior to German tanks at this time and had good armour protection and a good gun, but many of them lacked radios and had a one-gun turret in which the commander also had to load, aim and fire the main gun, a clearly impossible task.

In the late 1930s there had been many changes in the organisation of French armoured units and these were still

coming into effect at the time of the German invasion. French armoured units were never given the chance to prove their potential as they were usually employed without adequate artillery and infantry support, had poor communications, not only from tank to tank but also at higher levels, and were given few opportunities to carry out training before the war.

With proper tactical training and good command and control the French tanks could have been very effective in 1940. As it was they were frittered away in small local actions as the Blitzkrieg rolled over the country. If the French Division Legère Mechanique had been allowed to operate on its own, if it had had a proper system of supply, and if many other things too . . . then the French armoured troops could have shown their true ability, but they never had an opportunity.

With the fall of France many of the French tanks were taken over intact by the Germans; some were used in the tank role on the Eastern Front but many were converted into self-propelled guns that served with the German Army through to 1944/45.

Renault AMC 35 Light Tank

AMC 35 (ACG1), plus Belgian and German variants.
Country of origin: France.
Crew: 3.
Armament: One 47mm gun; one 7.5mm machine-gun co-axial with main armament.
Armour: 25mm (1in) maximum.
Dimensions: Length 15ft (4.572m); width 7ft 4in (2.235m); height 7ft 8in (2.336m).
Weight: 31,967lbs (14,500kg).
Engine: Renault four-cylinder petrol engine developing 180hp.
Performance: Maximum road speed 25mph (40km/h); range 100 miles (161km); vertical obstacle 2ft (0.609m); trench 6ft (1.828m); gradient 60 per cent.
History: In service with the French Army from 1935 to 1940. Also used by the Belgian and German Armies (see text).

As well as building a light tank to meet the AMR requirement (the Renault AMR 33 VM), Renault also built a tank to meet the AMC (*Auto-Mitrailleuse de Reconnaissance*) requirement. The first prototype, which was completed in 1933, had a turret from the Renault light tank, featuring a 37mm gun. Trials with this prototype were not satisfactory so a further prototype was built, under the designation AMC Renault 34 YR.

This was the first French light tank to have a two-man turret, at last enabling the tank commander to carry out his proper role, that is to command the tank, and not operate the armament. AMC 34 YR armament consisted of a 25mm gun and a co-axial 7.5mm machine-gun. It was powered by a Renault four-cylinder petrol engine which developed 120hp, giving the tank a maximum road speed of 25mph (40km/h). Combat weight was 10.63 tons (10,800kg).

This tank was followed by the Renault AMC 35 or ACG1, of which early models were built by Renault, but then the majority by AMX. The tank had a crew of three, with the driver at the front of the hull and the other two crew members in the turret. Armament consisted of a 47mm gun and a co-axial 7.5mm machine-gun, although some tanks had the 47mm gun replaced by a long barrelled 25mm anti-tank gun. The suspension was of the scissors type with horizontal springing. There were five road wheels on each side, with the drive sprocket at the front and the idler at the rear, and five track-return rollers.

Production of the AMC 35 amounted to about 100 tanks, of which 12 were purchased by the Belgians in 1937. The tanks were re-designated *Auto-Mitrailleuses de Corps de Cavalerie*, and had a turret of Belgian design and construction armed with a 47mm anti-tank gun and a co-axial 13.2mm machine-gun. After the fall of France some AMC 35s were taken over by the Germans, who called them the *PzKpfw* AMC 738 (*f*).

Above right: The three-crew AMC 35 was a significant departure from previous French de-signed tanks in that it had a two-man-turret.

Centre right: AMC 35 with its original short-barrelled 47mm gun replaced by a long-barrelled 25mm Hotchkiss anti-tank gun, but retaining co-axial machine gun.

Right: The AMC 35 was designed by Renault but later production was undertaken by AMX. This is the 47mm-gunned version which had a cast turret.

Hotchkiss H-35 and H-39 Light Tank

H-35, H-39 and German variants.
Country of origin: France.
Crew: 2.
Armament: One 37mm SA 38 gun; one 7.5mm Model 1931 machine-gun co-axial with main armament.
Armour: 40mm (1.57in) maximum; 12mm (0.47in) minimum.
Dimensions: Length 13ft 10in (4.22m); width 6ft 1in (1.85m); height 6ft 7in (2.14m).
Weight: Combat 26,456lbs (12,000kg).
Ground Pressure: 12.8lb/in^2 (0.90kg/cm^2).
Engine: Hotchkiss six-cylinder water-cooled petrol engine developing 120bhp at 2,800rpm.
Performance: Road speed 22.5mph (36km/h); range 93 miles (150km); vertical obstacle 1ft 8in (0.5m); trench 5ft 11in (1.8m); gradient 60 per cent.
History (H-35): Entered service with the French Army in 1936 and used until fall of France. Also used by Free French, Germany and Israel (after World War II). (Note: data relate to the H-39.)

When the first *DLM* (*Division Légère Mécanique*) was formed in 1934, the French Army wanted a light tank to operate with the *SOMUA* S-35 medium tank. In 1933 the French infantry ordered a light tank, the prototype of which ▶

Below: Side view of Hotchkiss H-39 light tank with a near horizontal rear engine deck as compared to the downward-sloping deck of the earlier Hotchkiss H-35. By the beginning of the war 821 H-35/H-39 tanks were in service with the French Army.

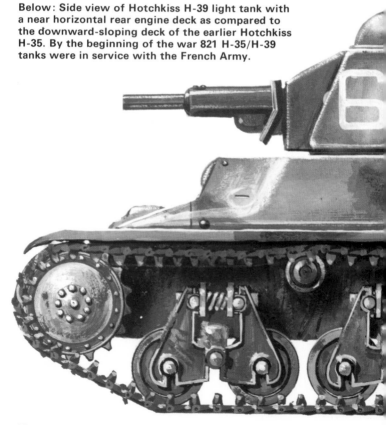

Above: Hotchkiss H-35 light tank armed with the short barrelled SA 18 37mm gun which had a muzzle velocity of 1,273fps (388m/s) compared to the more common SA 38 (33 calibre) long barrel weapon with a muzzle velocity of 2,300fps (701m/s). Some 100 rounds of 37mm and 2,400 rounds of 7.5mm machine gun ammunition were carried, with the empty cartridge cases for the latter being deposited outside via a chute.

was completed by Hotchkiss in 1934. This was rejected by the infantry in favour of the similar Renault 35 tank. The cavalry, however, accepted the tank for service as the *Char Léger* Hotchkiss *modèle* 35H, and in the end the infantry also accepted the tank for its *DCs* (*Divisions Cuirassées*) formed shortly before war broke out.

The H-35 weighed 11.22 tons (11,400 kg) and was powered by a six-cylinder petrol engine which developed 75bhp at 2,700rpm and gave the tank a top road speed of 17mph (28km/h). The H-35's maximum armour thickness was 34mm (1.34in). The H-35 was followed by the H-38 and the H-39, which had a number of modifications, including thicker armour and more powerful engines which increased their speed. Production of the H-35/H-39 family amounted to about 1,000 tanks, of which some 821 were in front-line service when World War II broke out.

The hull of the H-39 was of cast sections bolted together. The driver was seated at the front of the hull, slightly offset to the right, and was provided with a two-piece hatch cover, one part of which opened upwards and the other part forwards. A hull escape hatch was provided in the floor of the tank. The turret was also of cast construction and this was built by APX and was identical to that fitted to the Renault R-35 and R-40 tanks. The turret was provided with a cupola, which could be traversed, and the commander entered via a hatch in the turret rear, which also folded down horizontally to form a seat, this being used when the tank was not in action. The engine was at the rear of the hull on the left, with the fuel tank on the right, these being separated from the fighting compartment by a fireproof bulkhead. Compared with the earlier H-35, the deck of the H-39 was almost horizontal, the earlier model's deck having been more sloped. An external fuel tank could be fitted if required, as could a detachable skid tail, the latter being designed to increase the tank's cross-country performance. Power was transmitted to the gearbox and transmission at the front of the hull by a shaft. The suspension on each side comprised three bogies, each with two wheels. These were mounted on bellcranks with double springs between the upper arms. The drive sprocket was at the front and the idler at the rear; there were two track-return rollers. Main armament consisted of a 37mm gun with a 7.5mm machine-gun mounted co-axially to the right. Two different models of 37mm gun were fitted: the SA 38 with a long (33 calibre) barrel, giving a muzzle velocity of 2,300fps (701m/s), or the shorter SA 18 gun (21 calibre) with a muzzle velocity of 1,273fps (388m/s). The former was the more common weapon for the H-39. Some 100 rounds of 37mm and 2,400 rounds of 7.5mm

Above: Front and top views of H-39 light tank which, together with the H-35, was used in the cavalry role, or in a direct support role with the infantry.

Right: The H-35 tank, like many other French tanks, had the drawback of having a one-man turret.

machine-gun ammunition were carried. The empty cartridge cases for the latter went into a chute which deposited them outside of the tank. Like most French tanks of this period, the Hotchkiss H-35/H-39 had one major drawback, and this was that the commander also had to aim and load the gun.

When France fell the Germans took over many H-35 and H-39 tanks, some being used on the Russian Front without modification apart from the installation of a German radio and a new cupola. This had a flat roof and was provided with a two-piece hatch cover which opened to the left and right. Some were also provided with a searchlight over the main armament. The Germans also developed two self-propelled guns based on the Hotchkiss H-35 and H-39 chassis. The anti-tank model was known as the 7.5cm *Pak* 40 L/48 *auf Gw* 39H (*f*), and had its turret removed and replaced by an open-topped armoured superstructure mounted at the rear of the hull. In the front of this superstructure was mounted a 7.5cm anti-tank gun. Twenty-four such conversions were produced from 1942. This version weighed 12.3 tons (12,500kg) and had a crew of five. The second model was the 10.5cm *Panzer-feldhaubitze* 18 *auf Sfh* 39H (*f*) or 10.5cm *le FH* 18 *GW* 39H (*f*), 48 of these being built from 1942. This model was armed with a 10.5cm howitzer and was provided with a similar superstructure to the anti-tank model.

When the state of Israel was formed after the end of World War II, it could not obtain any modern tanks at all and had to rely on what equipment was left in the area after the war. These included some French H-39 tanks and a number of these were rearmed with British 6pounder anti-tank guns.

Char B1 Heavy Tank

***Char* B1, B1-*bis*, B1-*ter* and German variants.**
Country of origin: France.
Crew: 4.
Armament: One 75mm gun in hull; one 7.5mm machine-gun in hull; one 47mm turret-mounted gun; one 7.5mm machine-gun co-axial with 47mm gun (see text).
Armour: 60mm (2.36in) maximum.
Dimensions: Length 21ft 5in (6.52m); width 8ft 2in (2.5m); height 9ft 2in (2.79m).
Weight: Combat 70,548lbs (32,000kg).
Ground Pressure: 19.7lb/in^2 (1.39kg/cm^2).
Engine: Six-cylinder inline water-cooled petrol engine developing 307bhp at 1,900rpm.
Performance: Road speed 17mph (28km/h); range 93 miles (150km); vertical obstacle 3ft 1in (0.93m); trench 9ft (2.75m); gradient 50 per cent.
History: Entered service with the French Army in 1936 and used until fall of France in 1940. Also used by the German Army (see text).

In 1921 the *Section Technique des Chars de Combat*, under the leadership of the famous French exponent of armour, General Estienne, requested five companies to draw up a design for a tank weighing 14.75 tons (15,000kg), to be armed with a hull-mounted 47mm or 75mm gun. In 1924 four different mockups were presented at Rueil and three years later orders were given for the construction of three tanks, one each from FAMH (*Forges et Aciéries de la Marine et d'Homécourt*), FCM (*Forges et Chantiers de la Méditerranée*) and Renault/Schneider. These were completed between 1929 and 1931 and were known as the *Char* B. These weighed 24.6 tons (25,000kg) and were armed with a hull-mounted 75mm gun, two fixed machine-guns in the front of the hull, and two turret-mounted machine-guns. They had a crew of four. With modifications the type entered production as the *Char* B1, but only 35 of these had been built before it was decided to place in production an improved model with heavier armour and a more powerful engine, to be known as the *Char* B1-*bis*. Some 365 were built by the fall of France in 1940. Of these there were 66 *Char* B1-*bis* tanks in the 1st, 2nd, 3rd and 4th DCRs

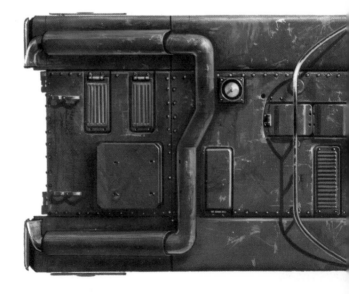

(*Division Cuirassées de Réserve*), and a further 57 in independent companies.

The *Char* B1-*bis* had excellent armour which could withstand attack from any German anti-tank gun except the famous 88mm. The hull of the tank was of cast sections bolted together. The driver was seated at the front of the hull on the left and steered the tank with a conventional steering wheel which was connected in turn to a hydrostatic system. Mounted to the driver's right was the 75mm SA 35 gun, which had a very short barrel (17.1 calibres), elevation being +25° and depression −15°. The gun was fixed in traverse and was aimed by the driver, who swung the tank until the gun was lined up with the target. An unusual feature of this gun was that an air compressor was provided to blow fumes out of the barrel. A 7.5mm Chatellerault machine-gun ▶

Right and below: Front and top views of the Char B1-bis. The main 75mm gun, to the right and below the driver, was operated by the driver. It was fixed and the driver had to aim it by pointing the entire tank at the target. Elevation was +25° and depression −15°. Ammunition for the weapons was stored on the walls and under the floor of the fighting compartment of the tank.

was fixed in the front of the hull on the right, lower than the 75mm gun. This machine-gun could be aimed by the driver or commander. The APX turret was identical to that installed on the SOMUA S-35 tank and was armed with a 37mm gun with an elevation of +18° and a depression of −18°. A 7.5mm machine-gun was also mounted in the turret, and this had an independent traverse of 10° left and 10° right. Some 74 rounds of 75mm (HE), 50 rounds of 47mm (AP and HE) and 5,100 rounds of machine-gun ammunition were carried.

The tank had a crew of four, the driver/gunner, wireless operator, loader and commander. The last had to aim, load and fire the turret guns as well as command the tank. The loader was just as busy, as he had to pass ammunition to the commander as well as load the hull-mounted 75mm gun. The wireless operator was seated near the turret. Normal means of entry and exit was via a large door in the right of the hull. The driver had a hatch over his position, and there was also a hatch in the turret rear on the right. There were two emergency exits, one in the floor of the tank and another hatch in the roof of the engine compartment. The engine, transmission and fuel tanks were at the

Above: The German Army removed the hull-mounted 75mm gun from a small number of Char B1 tanks and fitted a flame-thrower. These became known as PzKpfw B1 (f) Fahrschulewagen.

Right: A Char B1 knocked out in the summer of 1940. At that time the Char B1 was one of the most formidable tanks in service.

rear of the hull, and a compressed air starting system was fitted in addition to the normal electric starting system. Another interesting feature of the tank was the installation of a gyroscopic direction indicator, also driven by the compressor. The suspension on each side consisted of 16 double steel bogie wheels. Of these, three assemblies had four wheels each and these were controlled by vertically mounted coil springs and semi-elliptical leaf springs. There were also three independent bogie wheels forward and one to the rear, with quarter-elliptic leaf springs. The drive sprocket was at the rear and the idler at the front, the latter being coil sprung to act as the tensioner.

Further development of the *Char* B1-*bis* resulted in the *Char* B1-*ter*. This had additional armour, a fifth crew member (a mechanic) and the 75mm hull gun had a traverse of 5° left and 5° right. Only five of these were built and none was used in action. The tank was also used by the German Army for a variety of roles. The driver training model had the turret and hull-mounted gun removed, the latter being replaced by a machine-gun. The type was then known as the *PzKpfw* B1 (*f*) *Fahrschulewagen*. The Germans also modified 24 tanks in 1942–43 for use in the flamethrower role. These had flameguns fitted in place of the hull guns and the type was known as the *PzKpfw* B1-*bis* (*Flamm*). The gun turret was retained to give the vehicle some anti-tank capability. Finally there was a self-propelled gun model. This had the hull gun and turret removed, and on top of the tank was mounted a standard German 105mm howitzer. The conversion work was carried out by Rheinmetall-Borsig. Very few such conversions were effected and most of these served in France.

A few *Char* B1-*bis* tanks were used by the French when they liberated the port of Royan in 1944. The *Char* B1-*bis* would have probably been followed in production by the ARL 40 but this was still at the design stage when France fell. The type was eventually placed in production as the ARL 44 in 1946. The main other French infantry tanks (medium/heavy) were the *Char* D1 and *Char* D2. The *Char* D1 was developed in the early 1930s and 160 were built for the infantry between 1932 and 1935. These weighed 12.8 tons (13,000kg) and were armed with a turret-mounted 47mm gun and a fixed machine-gun in the front of the hull, fired by the driver. Later production models had thicker armour, a more powerful engine and a machine-gun mounted co-axially with the main armament. Before production of the D1 was even completed, work started on a more powerful and heavier armoured tank called the *Char* D2. This weighed 15.75 tons (16,000kg) and was powered by a six-cylinder petrol engine developing 150hp. By 1940 about 100 had been built.

Renault R-35 Light Tank

R-35 and German variants.
Country of origin: France.
Crew: 2.
Armament: One 37mm gun; one 7.5mm machine-gun co-axial with main armament.
Armour: 45mm (1.77in) maximum.
Dimensions: Length 13ft 10in (4.2m); width 6ft 1in (1.85m); height 7ft 9in (2.37m).
Weight: 22,046lbs (10,000kg).
Ground Pressure: 9.52lb/in^2 (0.67kg/cm^2).
Engine: Renault four-cylinder petrol engine developing 82bhp at 2,200rpm.
Performance: Road speed 12.42mph (20km/h); range 87 miles (140km); vertical obstacle 1ft 10in (0.5m); trench 5ft 3in (1.6m) or 6ft 7in (2m) with tail; gradient 60 per cent.
History: Entered service with the French Army in 1936 and used until fall of France. Also used by Germany, Italy (tanks received from Germany), Poland, Romania, Turkey and Yugoslavia.

In 1934 the French infantry issued a requirement for a new light tank to replace the large number of World War I Renault FT-17 two-man tanks which were still in service (these in fact remained in service with French Army until 1940, and with the German Army for some years later still). This new light tank was to weigh 7.87 tons (8,000kg), have a crew of two, a maximum road speed of 12.42mph (20km/h), be armed with twin 7.5mm machine-guns or a single 37mm gun, and have a maximum armour thickness of 40mm (1.57in). Four companies submitted designs: *Compagnie Général de Construction des Locomotives*, Delaunay-Belleville, FCM and Renault.

The Renault model, called the Renault ZM (or R-35) was selected for production and the first 300 were ordered in May 1935. The prototype was

Below: Side view of Renault R-35 light tank clearly showing the scissor-type suspension, common to many French tanks of this period, trailing idler wheel and the special tail that was fitted to enable the tank to cross wide trenches. It was one of the better French light tanks of the period.

armed with twin turret-mounted 7.5mm machine-guns and differed in many details to the production models. The suspension was based on that used in the Renault *Auto-Mitrailleuse de Reconnaissance* 1935 Type ZT (AMR) which had already been accepted for service. Production of the Renault R-35 amounted to between 1,600 and 1,900 tanks, and when war was declared this was the most numerous of all of the French tanks, and many were also exported. In May 1940 there were some 945 R-35/R-40 tanks in front line use, and of these 810 were organic to armies and another 135 were with the 4th *DCR* (*Division Cuirassée de Réserve*). Their role was the support of the infantry and their slow road speed gave them little strategic mobility.

The FCM entry in the original competition was also adopted for service as the *Char Léger Modèle* 1936 FCM, but only 100 were built by 1940 and these were sufficient to equip a mere two battalions. The FCM tank was faster than the R-35 and had a much larger radius of action. It was powered ▶

Above: Repairs had often to be accomplished in the field to allow the damaged AFVs to be returned to front line service as quickly as possible. Here, in a temporary field workshop, the front armour of a Renault R-35 light tank has been lifted off to allow repair work to be carried out on the differential and final drive assemblies. The R-35 was the most numerous of all French infantry tanks, but had a one-man turret and was very slow.

by a 90hp diesel and its suspension was similar to that used on the *Char* B1. Its hull was of welded construction and in this respect was quite advanced. Combat weight was about 10.33 tons (10,500kg). Some of these FCMs were converted to self-propelled guns after the German invasion.

Like most French tanks, the hull of the R-35 was of cast sections which were then bolted together. The driver was seated at the front of the hull, slightly offset to the left, and was provided with two hatch covers, one of which opened forwards and the other upwards, the operation of the latter being assisted by a hydraulic ram. The APX turret was in the centre of the hull and was identical to that installed on the Hotchkiss H-35 and H-39 tanks. This was provided with a cupola but the commander entered the turret via a hatch in the rear of the turret, and this hatch also acted as a seat for the commander when the tank was not in action. Main armament consisted of a 37mm SA 18 gun with a 7.5mm machine-gun mounted co-axially. Some 100 rounds of 37mm and 2,400 rounds of 7.5mm ammunition were carried. The empty cartridge cases from the machine-gun were deposited into a chute which carried them out through a hole in the floor of the tank. Late production tanks were armed with the long-barrelled SA 38 37mm gun. The engine was at the rear of the hull on the right, with the fuel tank (this being of the self-sealing type) on the left. A fireproof bulkhead separated the engine and fighting compartments. The suspension on each side consisted of five rubber-tired wheels, the first being mounted independently and the others on two bogies. These were mounted on bellcranks with springs. The drive sprocket was at the front and the idler at the rear, and there were three track-return rollers. Most tanks had a tail fitted to increase their trench-crossing capabilities. When first developed the tank was not provided with a radio, although these were fitted to late production tanks. This addition meant even more work for the commander, who already had to command the tank as well as aim, load and fire the armament.

Another development of the R-35 was the AMX-40. This had a new suspension designed by AMX, consisting of 12 small road wheels, with the drive sprocket at the front and the idler at the rear, and there were four track-return rollers. This suspension was an improvement over the Renault suspension. Two battalions were equipped with the AMX-40, or R-40 as the type was sometimes called. The R-35 was also used as a fascine carrier. This model had a frame running from the front of the hull over the turret to the rear, on top of which was carried a fascine for dropping into trenches. Some tanks were also provided with FCM turrets of cast or welded construction,

Left: The Germans fitted about 100 Renault R-35 tanks with a Czech 47mm anti-tank gun in place of the turret. These were known as the 4.7cm Pak(t) auf GW R35 (f), but were already obsolete by the time they entered service. Others were used as carriers for ammunition and a few were even fitted with a 105mm howitzer and designated leFH 18 auf GW 35R (f).

Above and left: Front and rear views of an R-35 tank. Playing card insignia were often painted on the turret for identification of sub-units. When open, the door in the turret rear provided a seat for the tank commander who also had to aim, load and fire the 37mm SA 18 gun and the co-axial machine-gun. Turret was the same as that fitted to the H-35/H-39 tanks.

although these were not adopted for service. Other trials versions included a mine-detection tank and a remote-controlled tank.

The Germans used the R-35 for various roles. The basic tank was used for the reconnaissance role on the Eastern Front from 1941 onwards under the designation *PzKpfw* R-35 (4.7cm). Many had their turrets removed and were used for towing artillery (*Traktor*) or for carrying ammunition, the latter version being known as the *Munitionpanzer* 35R (*f*). The anti-tank variant was known as the 4.7cm *Pak* (*t*) *auf GW* R35 (*f*), this consisting of an R-35 with its turret removed and replaced by a new open topped superstructure in the front of which was mounted a Czech 47mm anti-tank gun. About 100 of these were converted, but they were already obsolete by the time conversion work was completed. Alfred Becker fitted some with a 105mm howitzer and these were known as the 10.5cm *leFH* 18 *auf GW* 35R (*f*). Some examples, known as the *Mörserträger* 35R (*f*), were also fitted with an 80mm mortar.

Char Somua S-35 Medium Tank

S-35 and S-40.
Country of origin: France.
Crew: 3.
Armament: One 47mm gun; one 7.5mm Model 31 machine-gun co-axial with main armament.
Armour: 56mm (2.2in) maximum.
Dimensions: Length 17ft 11in (5.46m); width 6ft 11in (2.108m); height 8ft 10in (2.692m).
Weight: Combat 44,200lbs (20,048kg).
Ground Pressure: 13.08lb/in^2 (0.92kg/cm^2).
Engine: *SOMUA* eight-cylinder water-cooled petrol engine developing 190hp at 2,000rpm.
Performance: Maximum road speed 23mph (37km/h); road range 160 miles (257km); vertical obstacle 1ft 8in (0.508m); trench 7ft 8in (2.336m); gradient 65 per cent.
History: Entered service with the French Army in 1936 and used until fall of France in 1940. Also used by Germany and Italy (see text).

In the early 1930s the French cavalry issued a requirement for a tank to be called the AMC, or *Automitrailleuse de Combat*. A vehicle to this specification was built by *SOMUA* (*Société d'Outillage Mécanique et d'Usinage d'Artillerie*) at Saint Ouen. After trials this was accepted for service with the cavalry under the designation AMC *SOMUA* AC-3. Soon afterwards it was decided that the type would be adopted as the standard medium tank of the French Army, and it was redesignated the *Char* S-35, the 'S' standing for ▶

Below: Side view of Somua S-35 showing access doors in left side of hull. A hull escape hatch was also provided. The hull consisted of cast sections bolted together.

Above: The Char Somua S-35 medium tank was more than a match for any German tanks during the Battle of France in 1940, by which time some 500 had been built. The S-35 was well armed, had good mobility and firepower but, like most other French tanks of this period, the commander had to load, aim and fire the guns as well as command the tank. The turret of the S-35 was identical to that fitted to the Char B1-bis and D2 tanks and mounted a 47mm SA 35 gun and a 7.5mm Model 31 MG coaxial.

Above: After the fall of France in the summer of 1940, the occupying German forces took over all available French tanks and other weapons. This photograph shows a Somua S-35 medium tank leading Hotchkiss light tanks through Paris with their German crews. The Germans called the S-35 the PzKpfw 35C 739(f) and these were used on the Russian front. Some of these tanks were also supplied to the Italians.

SOMUA and the '35' for the year of introduction, 1935. About 500 had been built by the fall of France. Tank for tank, the S-35 was more than a match for any of the German tanks of that time, but bad tactics gave them little chance to prove their worth apart from a few isolated actions.

The S-35 had good armour, mobility and firepower, but it also had the usual French weakness in that the commander was also the gunner and loader. The hull was of three cast sections bolted together. These sections were the hull floor, front superstructure and rear superstructure, which were joined by bolts just above the tops of the tracks, with the vertical join between

Right and below:
Front, top and rear views of the Somua S-35 medium tank. The hull was cast in three sections and then bolted together just above the tops of the tracks. This proved one of the weak points as a hit on one of these joints generally split the tank wide open. The driver and radio operator, seated at the front, entered the tank through the door in the left side of the hull. The tank was well laid out, with ample vision devices provided. Note in particular the wide area of engine air-intake grilles at the rear, the shrouded turret machine gun, and the twin exhaust pipes running down the centre of the rear deck.

the front and rear parts near the rear of the turret. These joints were one of the weak points of the tank as a hit on one of these was likely to split the tank wide open. The hull had a maximum thickness of 1.6in (41mm). The driver was seated at the front of the hull on the left, and was provided with a hatch to his front. This hatch was normally left open as the tank moved up to the front. The radio operator was located to the right of the driver. Normal means of entry and exit for the driver and radio operator were through a door in the left side of the hull; a floor escape hatch was also provided for use in an emergency. The turret was also of cast construction and had a maximum ▶

thickness of 2.2in (56mm). It was identical with that fitted to the *Char* B1-*bis* and D2.

Main armament consisted of a 47mm SA 35 gun with an elevation of +18° and a depression of −18°, the turret being traversible through 360° by an electric motor. The 47mm gun could fire both HE and AP rounds with a maximum muzzle-velocity of 2,200fps (670m/s). A 7.5mm Model 31 machine-gun was mounted co-axially to the right of the main armament. This machine-gun was unusual in that it had a limited traverse of 10° left and 10° right of the main armament. Some 118 rounds of 47mm and 1,250 rounds of machine-gun ammunition were normally carried. Provision was also made for mounting another 7.5mm machine-gun on the commander's cupola for use in the anti-aircraft role. This last does not appear to have been fitted in action as no doubt the commander already had enough to do without having to cope with this weapon as well!

The engine and transmission were at the rear of the hull, with the engine on the left and the self-sealing petrol tank on the right. The engine compartment was separated from the fighting compartment by a fireproof bulkhead. The suspension on each side consisted of two assemblies, each of which had four bogie wheels mounted in pairs on articulated arms, these being controlled by semi-elliptic springs. The ninth bogie wheel at the rear was provided with its own spring. The idler was at the front and the drive sprocket at the rear, and there were two small track-return rollers. The lower part of the suspension was provided with an armoured cover which could be hinged up to allow access to the bogie assemblies.

In 1940 production of an improved model, the S-40 started. This had a more powerful 220hp engine and modified suspension, but few of these had been completed by the fall of France. Another interesting vehicle was the SAu 40 self-propelled gun, although this existed only in prototype form. This

Above: The final version of the Somua medium tank, considered by many to be the best French tank built, was the S-40. This had a more powerful 220hp engine and modified suspension, but few were built by the fall of France in 1940. This S-40 was captured by the Resistance towards the end of the war.

Right: A new S-40 on a low loader awaits delivery to the French Army. At one time it was thought that production for the French Army would be undertaken in the USA.

Above: A captured S-35 medium tank is used to patrol an airfield in occupied France. This photograph shows the use of the standard German wireless aerial base to turret rear.

had a hull-mounted 75mm gun to the right of the driver, and a different turret was fitted.

The S-35 was also used by the Germans for a variety of roles including crew training and internal security; some were even used on the Russian front. The Germans called the type the *PzKpfw* 35C 739 (*f*). Some were also fitted as command vehicles, and a few were handed over to the Italians.

GERMANY

The remarkable thing about the German use of tanks is that they ever managed to do it at all. During World War I, they did not produce a successful tank, unlike the French and British who employed tanks on a wide scale. And the Versailles Treaty of 1919 forbade the Germans from possessing any tanks, so any ideas their military thinkers did have suffered from not being put into practice (although some tanks were produced in Russia during the 1920s and tactics tried out with the Soviet Army, under great secrecy and to the advantage of both countries).

But the Germans had studied Liddell Hart and, when they defied the Treaty and started rearmament in 1933, tanks were high on the priority list. While Britain, France and other armies still tended to see the role of the tank as that of supporting infantry, Germany created the most success-ful formations of the time, based on the tank. The 1st Panzer Division was formed in 1935, with two battalions of tanks, two of infantry, two of artillery and one of motor-cycles, plus supporting units. By 1939 eight Panzer divisions had been formed, and these played a decisive role in the Blitzkrieg campaigns against Poland and France. These and subsequent campaigns demonstrated that armoured divisions had both greater striking power and greater mobility than infantry divisions on which armies had been based during and immediately after World War I.

When laying plans for production of his main battle tanks, Panzer virtuoso General Heinz Guderian foresaw

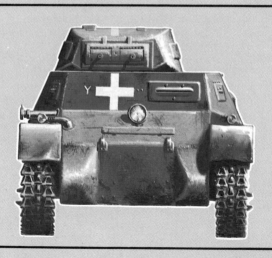

that the major battles would be fought with two types: the more numerous one carrying a high-velocity gun for anti-tank work, and a second acting as a support tank for the first, carrying a large-calibre gun capable firing a good high explosive (HE) shell. Panzer divisions saw action in all fronts from North Africa to Russia (but their tanks were not designed with the vast frozen wastes in mind). During the Blitzkrieg through France, many French tanks proved more than a match for the German counterparts, but the Germans used their armour more boldly, and thus more successfully. Having knocked out huge numbers of Soviet tanks during their advance into Russia, the German tanks (PzKpfw III and IV) once again met their betters in the T-34, which in effect changed all previous German tank specifications. It became obvious that what was needed was more speed, more armour (and sloped as much as possible) and a bigger gun. The result was the superb PzKpfw V Panther with its 75mm gun, and the two classic German "heavies", the Tiger I and Tiger II with 88mm guns.

One of the best advantages the Germans had over their enemies was that the Panzer masterminds never bothered with producing "infantry" tanks to co-operate with the footsloggers. One of the surprising disadvantages it experienced was that Hitler's war machine took such a long time to get organised, so that the Panther and Tiger were not ready in time, and the heavy tank losses generally could not be replaced quickly enough.

PzKpfw I Light Tank

SdKfz 101.
Country of origin: Germany.
Crew: 2.
Armament: Two 7.92mm MG 34 machine-guns.
Armour: 0.28in (7mm) minimum; 0.51in (13mm) maximum.
Dimensions: Length 13ft 3in (4.03m); width 6ft 9in (2.05m); height 5ft 8in (1.72m).
Weight: 11,905lbs (5,400kg).
Ground Pressure: 5.71lb/in^2 (0.4kg/cm^2).
Power to weight ratio: 11.32hp/ton.
Engine: Krupp M305 four-cylinder horizontally-opposed air-cooled petrol engine developing 60hp at 2,500rpm.
Performance: Road speed 23mph (37km/h); range 125 miles (200km); vertical obstacle 1ft 2in (0.355m); trench 4ft 7in (1.4m); gradient 58 per cent.
History: Served with the German Army from 1934 to 1941 as a tank, and to 1945 in other roles. Also used by Spain. (Note: Data relate to *PzKpfw* I A.)

In 1933, when Germany began openly to rearm, it was realised that the development of a full family of armoured vehicles would take several years. In the meantime it was decided to build light vehicles which the new armoured formations could use for training and experience. Contracts were therefore laid for a series of armoured vehicles between 3.9 and 6.9 tons (4,000 and 7,000kg) overall weight, and Krupp's design was the one chosen.

The *PzKpfw* I A was a small two-man tank which was inadequate in most respects even by the modest standards of the day. The hull was lightly armoured and had many openings, crevices and joints, all of which generally weakened it and made it vulnerable to attack. The engine was low powered and as a result performance was poor. The gearbox was a standard commercial crash type, with five forward speeds and one reverse. Fittings were minimal, and there was little evidence of designing for crew comfort. The suspension

Below: The PzKpfw Model B differed from the Model A in having a more powerful engine. This necessitated a longer hull. To compensate for the extra length an additional road wheel was fitted, the idler was raised off the ground and an extra return roller added.

showed evidence of plagiarisation of some of the features of the Carden-Loyd light tanks of the 1920s, in that an external beam carried the outer ends of the bogie axles and the rear idler. The drive-sprocket was at the front, which meant that the transmission train ran along the floor of the hull to a differential beside the driver's feet. Both driver and commander shared the same compartment, the driver climbing in through a hull door on the side, the commander using a large hatch in the turret roof. Since his vision was very restricted when the vehicle was closed down, the commander generally spent his time standing up with the upper half of his body well exposed. The ▶

Above: A PzKpfw Model B light tank in France in summer 1940. The first model was powered by a Krupp 60hp petrol engine but the Model B had the 100hp Maybach engine. This was a great improvement but the tank was still under-armed.

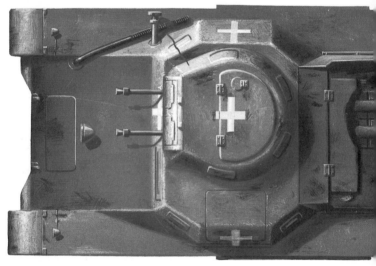

little turret was traversed by hand, and the commander fired the two machine-guns, for which there were 1,525 rounds of ammunition. The inadequacies of the Krupp engine became quickly apparent, and it was superseded by a more powerful one of 100bhp. This was a six-cylinder water-cooled inline Maybach, and to fit it in the chassis an extra 1ft 5in (43cm) of length had to be added to the hull. This brought about changes in the suspension, and an extra wheel station was added. In turn this lengthened the track in contact with the ground, and so the rear idler was lifted up. This was designated the *PzKpfw* 1 B, which was altogether a better vehicle, although it suffered from the same failings in armour and armament as did the 1A.

Over 2,000 IBs were built, reflecting the greater use that could be made of the more powerful model, and although only meant as interim vehicles until the proper battle tanks could be introduced, they were in action as early as 1936 in the Spanish Civil War, and after that in Poland, the Low Countries in 1940, Africa, Greece, the Balkans and even in Russia during 1941, though by then they were well out-dated and inadequate for anything except very minor tasks. In their early days these little tanks had survived very largely by virtue of the fact that there was no effective anti-tank armament in service with any army, and tanks were virtually immune to infantry weapons. However, as soon as any light guns could be brought to bear the *PzKpfw* I

Above: The PzKpfw Model A light tank was used in action for the first time during the Spanish Civil War, and later in Poland, Low Countries in 1940, Africa, Greece, Balkans and even during the early part of the Russian campaign. It was soon phased out of front line service as it lacked both armour and firepower and many were knocked out by the small British 2pounder anti-tank gun during the retreat to Dunkirk.

Left and above left: Top and front views of the PzKpfw I light tank which entered service with the German Army in 1934. Its two-man crew consisted of the driver and commander/gunner. Armament was of two 7.92mm MG 34 machine guns in a turret, offset to the right of the hull. Variants of the tank included a command vehicle and an ammunition carrier. A few were fitted with a 4.7cm anti-tank gun or a 15cm gun, but these conversions were not a great success as the chassis was overloaded.

was doomed, and many were destroyed by British 2pounder fire in the retreat to Dunkirk.

Several experiments were tried on the type, one such being the introduction of radio. This was only fitted to the IB version, and judging from photographs there was a sizeable proportion of each unit which could communicate by this means. The other vehicles watched for hand signals from their sub-unit leader. A successful variant to the basic tank was the conversion to a small command vehicle, an idea which started in 1936. By 1938 200 had been completed. The turret was replaced by a square full-width superstructure with a low square cupola on top. A single machine-gun was fitted for self-defence, and could be removed and set up on its ground mount. The crew was increased to three, and two radio sets were fitted. These vehicles were allotted to armoured units of all kinds, and altogether 96 of them saw action in France. Many others went to Russia in the following year, though they must have been terribly vulnerable to any form of effective fire.

A very small number of redundant *PzKpfw* Is were converted to other roles. A few were made into repair tractors, and others became ammunition carriers. About 200 were fitted with a 4.7cm gun and became light SP anti-tank guns; a very few others were fitted with 15cm guns, but in both cases the chassis was overloaded and the idea was dropped after limited use.

PzKpfw II Light Tank

***PzKpfw* II, or *SdKfz* 121 *Aust* A to F.**
Country of origin: Germany.
Crew: 3.
Armament: One 2cm *KwK* 30 or 38 gun; one 7.92mm MG 34 machine-gun
co-axial with main armament.
Armour: 0.39in (10mm) minimum; 1.18in (30mm) maximum in the *Ausf* A,
B and C; 0.57in (14.5mm) minimum; 1.38in (35mm) maximum in the *Ausf* F.
Weight: 20,944lbs (9,500kg).
Ground Pressure: 11.3lb/in² (0.8kg/cm²).
Power to weight ratio: 13.9hp/ton.
Engine: Maybach HL 62 TR six-cylinder water-cooled inline petrol engine
developing 130hp at 2,600rpm.
Performance: Road speed 25mph (40km/h); range 120 miles (192km);
vertical obstacle 1ft 5in (0.43m); trench 5ft 8in (1.72m); fording depth 3ft
(0.91m); gradient 50 per cent.
History: In service with the German Army from 1936 to 1943. Also used
by Spain.

From a 1934 specification, a *PzKpfw* II design by MAN was finally
selected. A number of prototypes was built, and some of them were sent to
Spain for full-scale trials in action. The first production models appeared in
1935, but deliveries were slow for the next 18 months as changes were made
in the design. The armour was increased in thickness, particularly in the front,
and some changes were made in the suspension. The weight increased by
nearly 1.95 tons (2,000kg), and experiments were made to improve the
engine horsepower. An extra 10hp was found by boring out the cylinders of
the Maybach engine, though the lower power motor appears to have
continued to be fitted to some versions.

The three variants of the *PzKpfw* II, the *Ausf* A, B and C, were all very
similar, with only minor dimensional differences. The *Ausf* A had the original
low power engine and weighed 16,105lbs (7,305kg). About 100 were built
in 1935 and 1936. The *Ausf* B featured the higher power engine, new
reduction gears and tracks, and again the weight increased. The *Ausf* C

appeared in 1937 and carried thicker front armour, bringing the weight up to the final figure of 20,944lbs (9,500kg). Issues to units began in earnest in 1937, and by 1939 there were sufficient for over 1,000 to take part in the Polish campaign. Manufacture of the general type continued up to late 1942 or early 1943, by which time the basic tank was well outdated.

The hull was built up from welded heat-treated steel, 1.18in (30mm) thick on the front and 0.39in (10mm) on the sides and rear. The turret was made in a similar way, again 1.18in (30mm) thick on the front and 0.63in (16mm) around the sides and back. The engine was in the rear compartment, driving forward through the fighting compartment to a gearbox and final drive in front. The gearbox was a ZF crash-type with six forward speeds and one reverse, the steering being by clutches and brakes. The driver sat off-centre to the left side. The fighting compartment had the turret above it, again offset slightly to the left. The armament was an improvement on that of the *PzKpfw I*, but still not very effective: the 2cm gun had a maximum range of 656 yards (600m), and only fired armour-piercing ammunition, but it had a reasonably rapid rate of fire. Some 180 2cm and 1,425 7.92mm rounds were carried. However, armour penetration of these 2cm rounds was not impressive. Once again, vision was poor from the turret, and fire-control difficult when fully closed-down. Most vehicles seem to have had radio. The suspension was distinctive. There were five road wheels hung on quarter-elliptic leaf springs, with the rear idler and front drive sprocket both clear of the ground. This suspension was quite effective, and within the limits of its engine power the *PzKpfw II* was quite manoeuvrable and agile. The tracks were narrow, but apparently quite strong.

Despite the limitations of the design, the *PzKpfw II* formed the backbone of the armoured divisions of the German Army, and as late as April 1942 860 were still on strength. An attempt to improve the performance was made in late 1940 with the F variant. Thicker armour was fitted to the front and sides and a higher velocity gun installed, though its calibre was still only 2cm. However these changes did little to increase the battlefield value of the tank, and the extra 2,204lbs (1,000kg) of weight that they entailed put an extra strain on the engine. The basic chassis was used for several different special-purpose vehicles, and also as a test-bed for a variety of ideas, including the use of torsion-bar suspension systems. Some were turned into flamethrower vehicles, capable of about 80 shots of 2 to 3 seconds duration.

Left: PzKpfw II Ausf F light tank of a regimental H.Q. (indicated by the letter R on the turret side). The figures 06 identify the tank as part of a reconnaissance Zug. This actual tank was captured in North Africa and is now displayed at the Royal Armoured Corps Tank Museum at Bovington Camp, Dorset, England. The specification for the tank was issued in 1934 and prototypes were built by Henschel, Krupp and MAN. The latter was selected for production and first models were completed the following year. By May 1940 the German Army had 955 PzKpfw II tanks and this had risen to 1,067 vehicles by the following year.

PzKpfw III Battle Tank

PzKpfw III, or SdKfz 141, Ausf A to N.
Country of origin: Germany.
Crew: 5.
Armament: *Ausf* A, B, C and D one 3.7cm *KwK* L/45 gun, two 7.92mm MG 34 machine-guns co-axial with main armament; one 7.92mm MG 34 machine-gun in hull.
Ausf E, F, G and H one 5cm *KwK* 39 L/42 gun; one 7.92mm MG 34 machine-gun co-axial with main armament; one 7.92mm MG 34 machine-gun in hull.
Ausf J and L one 5cm *KwK* 39 L/60 gun; one 7.92mm MG 34 machine-gun co-axial with main armament; one 7.92mm MG 34 machine-gun in hull.
Ausf M and N one 7.5cm *KwK* L/24 gun; one 7.92mm MG 34 machine-gun co-axial with main armament; one 7.92mm MG 34 machine-gun in hull.
Armour: *Ausf* A, B and C 0.57in (14.5mm) minimum; 3.54in (90mm) maximum. *Ausf* D to G 1.18 (30mm) minimum; 3.54in (90mm) maximum. *Ausf* H to N 1.18in (30mm) minimum; 3.15in (80mm) maximum, but often seen with additional plate and spaced armour.
Dimensions: Length *Ausf* A and B 18ft 6in (5.7m); *Ausf* D to G 17ft 8in (5.4m); *Ausf* H 18ft 1in (5.52m); *Ausf* J to N 21ft 1in (6.4m).
Width *Ausf* A to C 9ft 2in (2.8m); *Ausf* D to G 9ft 6in (2.9m); *Ausf* H to N 9ft 8in (2.95m).
Height *Ausf* A 7ft 7in (2.35m); *Ausf* B and C 8ft 4in (2.55m); *Ausf* D to G 8ft (2.4m); *Ausf* H to N 9ft 8in (2.95m).
Weight: *Ausf* A to C 33,069lbs (15,000kg); *Ausf* D and E 42,769lbs (19,400kg); *Ausf* F and G 44,753lbs (20,300kg); *Ausf* H 47,619lbs (21,600kg); *Ausf* J to N 49,163lbs (22,300kg).
Ground Pressure: *Ausf* A to C 15.3lb/in^2 (0.973kg/cm^2); *Ausf* D 13.2lb/in^2 (0.93kg/cm^2); *Ausf* E and H to N 13.5lb/in^2 (0.95kg/cm^2); *Ausf* F and G 14.1lb/in^2 (0.99kg/cm^2).
Power to weight ratio: *Ausf* A to C 15.58hp/ton; *Ausf* D 16.75hp/ton; *Ausf* E and H to N 15.71hp/ton; *Ausf* F and G 15hp/ton.
Engine: *Ausf* A to C Maybach HL 108 TR V-12 water-cooled inline petrol engine developing 230hp at 2,600rpm; *Ausf* D Maybach HL 120 TR developing 320hp at 3,000rpm; *Ausf* E to N Maybach HL 120 TRM developing 300hp at 3,000rpm.
Performance: Road speed *Ausf* A to C 20mph (32km/h); *Ausf* E to N 25mph (40km/h). Cross-country speed all models 11mph (18km/h). Range *Ausf* A to C 94 miles (150km); *Ausf* D 103 miles (165km); *Ausf* E to N 109 miles (175km). Vertical obstacle all models 2ft (0.6m). Trench *Ausf* A to G 7ft 6in (2.3m). Fording depth *Ausf* A to J 2ft 7in (0.8m); *Ausf* L to N 4ft 3in (1.3m). Gradient 30 degrees.

Above: A PzKpfw III crew member surrenders to British infantry on 29 October 1942, during the North African campaign.

History: In service with the German Army from 1939 to 1945. Also used by Spain and Turkey.

In 1935, having gained some experience with the small tanks of that time, the Germans began to draw up specifications for their main battle tanks. The intention, as stated by General Guderian, was to have two basic types, the first carrying a high velocity gun for anti-tank work, backed up by machine- ▶

**Right and below:
Front, rear and side
views of a PzKpfw
III Ausf J of 3rd
Panzer Division on
the Russian Front
in 1941. The tank is
armed with a 50mm
KwK L/42 low
velocity gun for
which 78 rounds of
ammunition were
carried. On top of
the hull rear are
two sets of
replacement road
wheels.**

guns, and the second, a support tank for the first, carrying a large-calibre gun capable of firing a destructive HE shell. The intention was to equip the tank battalions with these in the ratio of three companies of the first type to one company of the support vehicles.

The *PzKpfw* III was the first of these two vehicles, and originally a high-velocity 5cm gun was called for. But the infantry were being equipped with the 3.7cm anti-tank gun, and it was felt that in the interest of standardisation the tanks should carry the same. However, a large turret ring was retained so that the vehicle could be up-gunned later without much difficulty. This was an important consideration and it undoubtedly enabled the *PzKpfw* III to remain in service for at least two years longer than would otherwise have been the case. The specification called for a weight of 14.76 tons (15,000kg), which was never achieved, and the upper limit had to be set at 23.62 tons (24,000kg) in deference to German road bridges.

The first prototypes appeared in 1936, and Daimler-Benz was chosen to be the main contractor. The *Ausf* A, B, C and D all appeared during the development phase, and were only produced in comparatively small numbers, and all were used to try out the different aspects of the design. The *Ausf* E became the production version, and was accepted in September 1939 as the *Panzerkampfwagen* III (3.7cm) (*SdKfz* 141). Production was spread among ▶

Right: A feature of the PzKpfw III was the prominent cupola at the rear of the turret which gave the commander very good all-round observation. This particular tank has spaced armour added across the front of the superstructure and across the mantlet front. Note the spare track links fixed under the nose.

Below: The PzKpfw III was originally armed with a 37mm gun but it was progressively upgunned to 50mm and finally to 75mm.

several firms, none of whom had had any previous experience of mass-producing vehicles — a fact which was to cause some trouble later on. The *PzKpfw* III *Ausf* E now formed the basis of the armoured divisions of the *Wehrmacht*. Some 98 were available for the invasion of Poland, and 350 took part in the Battle for France in May 1940. These tanks were mainly *Ausf* E, but there was still a number of earlier marks in service.

All versions featured a good crew layout. There was room for every man to do his job, and the prominent 'dustbin' cupola at the rear of the turret gave the commander an excellent view. The driver was assisted by a pre-selector gearbox giving him ten forward speeds and one reverse. The gearbox was rather complicated, and maintenance was difficult, but gear changing was easy and driving far less tiring than in many contemporary tanks at that time. The 320hp from the Maybach engine was adequate, if not exactly generous, and cross-country performance reasonably good. However, the tank was not entirely successful in action. The 3.7cm gun was not good enough to penetrate the armour of the British infantry tanks in France, and the 1.18in (30mm) of frontal armour could not keep out 2pounder shot. The same happened in the Western Desert when the *PzKpfw* III first went out with the *Afrika Korps*, but a new Krupp 5cm gun was rushed into production in late 1939 and was fitted to the *Ausf* E to H. This gun was not entirely satisfactory either as it was a low-velocity weapon, but it fired a useful HE shell and could outrange the British 2pounder. Some 99 rounds of 5cm ammunition and 2,000 of 7.92mm ammunition were carried.

A steady programme of improvement and development was now applied to the *PzKpfw* III. The *Ausf* H introduced extra armour bolted on to the hull and turret, and the tracks were widened to carry the extra weight. The complicated ten-speed gearbox was replaced by a simple six-speed manual change, and some of these features were retrofitted to earlier marks.

By 1941 there were nearly 1,500 *PzKpfw* IIIs in service, and the type was very successful in the first stages of the invasion of Russia. But the T-34 and KV tanks were impervious to the 5cm low-velocity gun, and in a crash programme a high-velocity version was introduced, though even this soon proved to be inadequate on the Eastern Front. However, it did well in the desert. Improved versions were now being designed fast. Production of the *PzKpfw* III had never reached the intended numbers (indeed it never did) and the J version, which carried 78 5cm rounds, was meant to be easier to produce and at the same time to provide better protection. The M went a bit further and also cut out many minor items such as hatches and vision ports. Some 2,600 were built in 1942, but already the tank was being outmoded and the N version carried a low-velocity 7.5cm gun to provide HE support to the heavy tank battalions. Some 64 7.5cm and 3,450 7.92mm rounds of ammunition were carried.

Below: A PzKpfw III with additional armour to hull front and mantlet, armed with a short-barrelled 7.5cm L/24 gun. Flame-thrower versions of the tank were in service by 1943.

Above: Supporting infantry, a PzKpfw III Ausf J acts as protection against enemy fire during the advance on Moscow in 1942. The PzKpfw III was the backbone of the Panzer Divisions in the early stages of the Russian campaign but could not seriously trouble the Soviet T-34 and KV tanks. It was replaced by later models of the PzKpfw IV.

Below: Apparently in the heat of battle, a PzKpfw III, again with additional armour to hull front and mantlet and the short-barrelled 7.5cm L/24 gun.

PzKpfw IV Medium Tank

***SdKfz*161.**
Country of origin: Germany.
Crew: 5.
Armament: One 7.5cm *KwK* L/24 gun; one 7.92mm MG 34 machine-gun co-axial with main armament; one 7.92mm MG 34 machine-gun in hull.
Armour: 0.79in (20mm) minimum; 3.54in (90mm) maximum.
Dimensions: Length 19ft 5in (5.91m); width 9ft 7in (2.92m); height 8ft 6in (2.59m).
Weight: 43,431lbs (19,700kg).
Ground Pressure: 10.6lb/in² (0.75kg/cm²).
Power to weight ratio: 15.5hp/ton.
Engine: Maybach HL 120 TRM V-12 inline diesel developing 300hp at 3,000rpm.
Performance: Road speed 25mph (40km/h); cross-country speed 12.5mph (20km/h); range 125 miles (200km); vertical obstacle 2ft (0.6m); trench 7ft 6in (2.3m); fording depth 2ft 7in (0.8m); gradient 30 degrees.
History: In service with the German Army from 1936 to 1945. Also used by Italy, Spain and Turkey. Last used by Syria in 1967. (Note: Data relate to the *PzKpfw* IV *Ausf* D.)

The *PzKpfw* IV was the only German tank to stay in continuous production throughout World War II, and it was probably in production longer than any other tank from that war, with the exception of the T-34. It began with the German specifications of 1935 in which it was foreseen that the main battle would be fought with two types, the more numerous one carrying a high-velocity gun (the *PzKpfw* III) and a support tank carrying a large-calibre gun firing a good HE shell. This was the *PzKpfw* IV. The gun chosen from the beginning was the 7.5cm short-barrelled *KwK*, and the tank was not to ▶

Below: Front view of a PzKpfw IV Ausf F2 of the Afrika Korps armed with the long barrelled 75mm KwK L/43 gun. This was encountered by the British in the Western Desert and called the 'Pz IV Special'. The fitting of this gun changed the role of the tank from that of a close support vehicle to a tank that could engage and defeat other tanks.

Right: Front view of PzKpfw IV Ausf A of 1st Panzer Division.

Above: PzKpfw IV Ausf H with long-barrelled L/48 gun, apron armour 5mm thick for the hull and 8mm thick on the turret. 'Zimmerit' anti-magnetic paste was usually applied to these vehicles to prevent magnetic charges from being attached.

Right: Disabled PzKpfw IV Ausf H tanks on the Voronezh Front in 1943. Note the skirt armour plates on the front tank; called Schurzen, they were 5mm thick and were intended to detonate HEAT projectiles prematurely. The detachable hull plates were often lost in the heat of battle but the turret plates were a permanent fixture. By the end of World War II 8,000 IVs had been built and it was the only German tank to remain in production all through the war. Some were even used as recently as 1967 by the Syrian Army in the static anti-tank role.

exceed 23.62 tons (24,000kg) in overall weight. In fact the specification called for a very similar vehicle to the *PzKpfw* III, and the layout of both was much the same, as were their tasks. Contracts were laid with a variety of firms, and there was the same fairly extended development time while the different designs were refined. It was 1939 before deliveries could be made in any quantity, and by that time the models had progressed to the Type D. This was the model which took part in the Polish and French campaigns, finally advancing into Russia in 1941, when its deficiencies became too apparent to be ignored further.

The Type D was slightly larger than the *PzKpfw* III, but had the same thin hull form and general shape. There were three compartments for the crew, the driver and radio operator occupying the front, with the hull machine-gun on the right side and set slightly back from the driver. In the fighting compartment the turret contained the commander, gunner and loader. The turret itself was traversed by an electric motor, whereas that of the *PzKpfw* III was hand-operated. The commander had a prominent cupola at the rear of the turret, and good all-round vision. There were escape hatches in the turret sides. The engine was in the rear compartment, and was the same as that of the *PzKpfw* III, although the layout of the ancillaries was slightly different. The drive ran forward to a front gearbox and sprocket. Suspension was by four coupled bogies on each side, sprung by leaf springs. There was a large idler wheel at the back and four small return rollers. There was room enough in the hull for 80 rounds of ammunition for the gun, and 2,800 rounds in belts for the machine-guns.

Battle experience soon showed that in this form the tank was a sound design and well laid out, but the armour was too thin for it to be able to

perform its proper task of supporting the *PzKpfw* IIIs as it had scarcely any advantage over any other tank. There followed a steady programme of improvement which was to continue until the end of the war. The next model, the E, was given thicker armour on the nose and turret, and a new cupola. Older models were retrofitted, which confuses precise identification of many photographs today. The F model was intended to be the main production version, though it too was soon overtaken, and a long-barrelled version of the 7.5cm gun was fitted. This long gun completely changed the role of the vehicle as it now became a fighting tank and began to take over that duty from the *PzKpfw* III from about mid-1941 onwards. The F was made in large numbers and fought on all fronts, as did the G which came soon after it, differing outwardly only in respect of its thicker armour and side skirting plates.

In 1943 another lease of life was injected by fitting the more powerful 7.5cm *KwK* 40 L/48 which enabled the *PzKpfw* IV to take on almost any tank in the world, and to give a good account of itself against the T-34. These larger guns had of course changed the turret, which from the G onwards was protected with extra plates, making it appear much longer at the rear. Large 0.2in (5mm) skirting plates hung over the sides and radically altered the look of the tank, making it appear deep and rather clumsy.

The last model was the J, which came out in 1944. By this time many raw materials were scarce and the design had to be simplified, but it was still basically the tank which had started the war five years before. By 1945 over 8,000 had been delivered and many more were built for specialist purposes. A few were still in service with the Syrian Army in the Arab-Israeli War of 1967, and apparently went well.

PzKpfw VI Tiger I Heavy Battle Tank

PzKpfw VI Tiger I, or *SdKfz* 181.
Country of origin: Germany.
Crew: 5.
Armament: One 8.8cm *KwK* 36 L/56 gun; one 7.92mm MG 34 machine-gun co-axial with main armament; one 7.92mm MG 34 machine-gun in hull.
Armour: 1.02in (26mm) minimum; 4.33in (110mm) maximum.
Dimensions: Length 27ft (8.25m); width 12ft 3in (3.73m); height 9ft 4in (2.85m).
Weight: 121,253lbs (55,000kg).
Ground Pressure: 14.8lb/in^2 (1.04kg/cm^2).
Power to weight ratio: 12.93hp/ton.
Engine: Maybach HL 230 P 45 V-12 water-cooled inline petrol engine developing 700bhp at 3,000rpm.
Performance: Road speed 24mph (38km/h); cross-country speed 12mph (20km/h); range 62 miles (100km); vertical obstacle 2ft 7in (0.8m); trench 5ft 11in (1.8m); fording depth 4ft (1.2m); gradient 35 degrees.
History: In service with the German Army from 1942 to 1945. (Note: Data relate to the Tiger I *Ausf* E.)

Below and right: Four views of the PzKpfw VI Tiger (Model H) of the 1st SS Panzer Division, 'Leibstandarte Adolf Hitler', as used on the Russian Front. The bands around the barrel of the 88mm KwK L/56 gun indicate the number of enemy tanks killed.

Despite the decision to mass produce the *PzKpfw* III and IV, and the fair certainty at the time that these two models would be adequate for the expected battles of the future, the German general staff also called for an even heavier tank in 1937. This was to be of 29.53 tons (30,000kg) or more and was to be a heavy 'breakthrough' tank to lead the armoured assaults. The design lapsed until 1941, by when it was realised that the *PzKpfw* IIIs and IVs had been less successful than had been expected against the heavily armoured French and British tanks in 1940. This view was fully endorsed when the Soviet T-34s and KV-Is were met later in 1941, and resulted in a specification for a heavy tank capable of mounting the highly successful 8.8cm high-velocity gun in a turret with full traverse and carrying sufficient armour to defeat all present and future anti-tank weapons.

Two firms submitted prototypes, using some of the developments from the 1937 ideas. These were Porsche and Henschel. The turret was common to both and came from Krupp. The Porsche design was unconventional and was not accepted, although it became a self-propelled gun. The Henschel design was relatively conventional, was obviously easier to make, and was thus accepted. This was given the designation *PzKpfw* VI and the name Tiger. Production began slowly in August 1942.

At the time of its introduction, and for some time afterwards, the Tiger was the most powerful tank in the world. The 8.8cm gun, which had 92 rounds of ammunition, was enormously formidable, and the armour ensured that any frontal shot could not penetrate. So effective was it that the Allies had to ▶

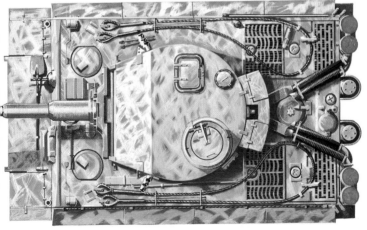

evolve special tactics to cope with it, though there were occasions when the tank was used so ineffectively that it never realised its potential. The Tiger was intended to be deployed in special battalions of 30 vehicles under the control of an army or corps headquarters. In general, this was done, though some armoured divisions were given their own Tiger battalions, particularly those of the *Waffen*-SS. Hitler had taken a personal interest in the Tiger, and he pressed for its use at the earliest opportunity. They were thrown into battle near Leningrad in the late summer of 1942, well spread out and in small numbers on poor ground. The result was a fiasco, as was the Kursk battle next year. But when used in ambush, where its gun could inflict the most damage, and where the heavy armour allowed a phased withdrawal, the Tiger was supreme. Indeed, in 1944 one solitary Tiger held up an entire division in France, and knocked out 25 Allied tanks before being stalked and destroyed.

The hull of the Tiger was a comparatively simple welded unit with a one-piece superstructure welded on top. The armour was not well sloped, but was thick. At the front it was 3.94in (100mm), around the sides 3.15in (80mm) and 1.02in (26mm) on the decks. To assist production all shapes were kept simple, and a long box-like side pannier ran along the top of the tracks. The turret was also simple, and the sides were almost upright. The mantlet was very heavy, with 4.33in (110mm) of armour, and carried the long and heavy gun. The turret traverse was very low-geared and driven by a hydraulic motor which took its power from the gearbox. Thus when the main engine was stopped, the turret had to be traversed by hand. The engine was changed in late 1943 to one of slightly greater power, but in general it was reliable and powerful enough.

The difficulty was that the tank's range was always too limited for operations, and top speed was low because of the need to gear down the transmission. The weight was too great for the usual German clutch and brake steering and Henschel adapted the British Merritt-Brown regenerative unit and coupled it to a pre-selector Maybach gearbox with eight forward speeds. The result was a set of controls which were very light for the driver,

but by no means easy to maintain or repair. The suspension was formed by overlapping road wheels; it was the first German tank to carry this distinctive feature, which gave a soft and stable ride. There were no less than eight torsion-bars on each side, and the floor was tightly packed with them. The difficulty with the overlapping wheels was that in the Russian winter nights they froze together and jammed the tracks, and the Russians often timed their attacks for dawn, when they could be sure of the Tigers being immobilised. The tracks were too wide for rail transport, and narrower ones were fitted for normal road and railway transport, when the outer set of road wheels was also removed.

The crew were housed in four compartments in the hull, the driver and hull gunner being separated in front, with the gearbox between them. The turret was fairly normal, though there was little room to spare when 92 rounds of 8.8cm ammunition were fully stowed. The gun was balanced by a heavy spring in a tube on the left of the turret. The 8.8cm shell could penetrate 4.4in (112mm) of armour at 492 yards (450m), which was more than enough for the armoured vehicles of the day. It was much feared by the crews of the comparatively vulnerable Shermans, the main Allied tank.

The Tiger was reasonably compact, but it was very heavy. It could not cross German bridges, and the first 400 models were capable of wading through deep rivers when they came to them. The necessity of fitting and re-fitting special tracks for rail travel was tedious, and the road wheels gave trouble from overloading. More nimble Allied tanks found that they could outmanoeuvre the Tiger and attack it from the rear, and these, together with the other limitations, caused it to be phased out in 1944. By August of that year 1,300 had been made, not many in view of their reputation and effect on Allied morale.

Below: Tiger (Model E) captured by the British in Tunisia. The British first encountered the Tiger in February 1943 near Pont du Fahs in Tunisia, when 6-pounders engaged two Tigers and nine PzKpfw IIIs and IVs. Both Tigers were knocked out at 500 yards.

PzKpfw V Panther Battle Tank

Panzerkampfwagen V, or *SdKfz* 171.
Country of origin: Germany.
Crew: 5.
Armament: One 7.5cm *KwK* 42 L/70 gun; two 7.92mm MG 34 machine-guns.
Armour: 0.6in (20mm) minimum; 4.72in (120mm) maximum.
Dimensions: Length 22ft 6in (6.68m); width 10ft 10in (3.3m); height 9ft 8in (2.95m). (Dimensional data relate to the *Ausf* G.)
Weight: 98,766lbs (44,800kg).
Ground Pressure: 12.5lb/in² (0.88kg/cm²).
Power to weight ratio: 15.9hp/ton.
Engine: Maybach HL 230 P 30 V-12 water-cooled petrol engine developing 700bhp at 3,000rpm.
Performance: Road speed 29mph (46km/h); cross-country speed 15mph (24km/h); range 110 miles (177km); vertical obstacle 3ft (0.9m); trench 6ft 3in (1.9m); fording depth 4ft 7in (1.4m); gradient 35 degrees.
History: In service with the German Army from 1943 to 1945. Also used by the Soviet Union and France after the war.

Left and below: Front, rear and side views of the PzKpfw V Panther, one of the best tanks of World War II. It was designed around the general concept of the Soviet T-34 tank, first seen in 1941.

Above: The PzKpfw V Panther featured well sloped armour, low turret-mounted 7.5cm KwK 42 L/70 gun, two 7.92mm MG 34 MGs and interleaved suspension that caused problems in the winter.

Until the invasion of Soviet Russia, the *PzKpfw* IV had been the heaviest tank in the German Army, and had proved quite adequate. In early October 1941 the new Soviet T-34 appeared and proved the *PzKpfw* IV to be completely out of date. The sloped armour, speed and manoeuvrability of the T-34 brought about a profound change of heart on the part of the Germans, and a new requirement was hurriedly drawn up. At first, to save time, it was even considered that the T-34 should be copied directly, but national pride forbade this approach and the specification issued in January 1942 merely incorporated all the T-34 features.

Designs were submitted in April 1942, and the first trial models appeared in September, the MAN design being chosen for production. There were the usual multitude of modifications called for as a result of the prototype's ▶

Above: The Panther tank was first committed to action during the Battle of Kursk in July 1943 and proved to be very unreliable. Many tanks broke down before they reached the front. There were problems with the engine, transmission and suspension, but once these were overcome the Panther became very popular with crews and was equal to the dreaded Soviet T-34 tank.

Above right: Panthers were built by MAN and Daimler-Benz, and by the end of the war over 5,000 had been built. But production never reached the 600 tanks a month demanded by Hitler in 1943.

performance, and spurred on by Hitler himself, MAN brought out the first production tank in January 1943, but Daimler-Benz had to be brought in to help. From then on production forged ahead, but never reached the ambitious target of 600 vehicles a month set by Hitler. There were many difficulties. The engine and transmission were overstressed to cope with the increase in weight, cooling was inadequate, engines caught fire, and the wheel rims gave trouble. When the Panther first went into action at Kursk in July 1943, it was at Hitler's insistence, and it was a failure. Most broke down on the journey from the railhead, and few survived the first day. All that were salvaged had to be sent back to the factory to be rebuilt. Later models corrected the faults, and the Panther soon became a fine tank which was superior to the T-34/76 and very popular with its crews.

The hull was fairly conventional in the German fashion, with a large one-piece glacis plate in which were originally two holes, one for the gunner and one for the driver. The G model had only the gun hole, the driver using a periscope. The turret was well sloped, although rather cramped inside, but

the commander was given a good cupola. The mantlet was massive, with tiny holes for the machine-gun and the gunner's binocular sight. From the front the protection was excellent. The suspension was by inter-leaved bogies sprung on torsion bars and it gave the Panther the best arrangement of any German tank of the war. The trouble was that the bogies could freeze up when clogged with snow in Russian winters, and so immobilise the vehicle. Maintenance was also difficult since the outer wheels had to be removed to allow access to the inner ones. Steering was by hydraulically operated disc brakes and epicyclic gears to each track, which allowed the tracks to be stopped separately when required without loss of power. It was an adaption of the Merritt-Brown system, but rather more complicated in design. The long 75mm gun (with 79 rounds) could penetrate 4.72in (120mm) of sloped plate at 1,094 yards (1000m) and this, together with the protection of the thick frontal armour, meant that the Panther could stand off from Allied tanks and knock them out without being harmed itself. The US Army reckoned that it took five Shermans to knock out one Panther and over 5,000 Panthers had been built by the end of the war. After 1943 the Germans needed numbers of tanks rather than improved designs, and the Panther was simplified to ease production. The hull sides were sloped more, the mantlet was thickened to prevent shot being deflected into the decking, and the gearbox was improved to cope with the weight problem.

Despite its complexity and high manufacturing cost, the Panther was a successful design and many consider it to have been one of the best tanks produced during the war. Towards the end of the war its petrol engine and complications were distinct disadvantages, but it was a powerful supplement to the *PzKpfw* IVs of the armoured formations, and it was really only defeated by the overwhelming Allied air strength.

PzKpfw VI Tiger II
Heavy Battle Tank

***PzKpfw* VI Tiger II, or *SdKfz* 182.**
Country of origin: Germany.
Crew: 5.
Armament: One 8.8cm *KwK* 43 L/71 gun; two 7.92mm MG 34 machine-guns.
Armour: 1.57in (40mm) minimum; 7.28in (185mm) maximum.
Dimensions: Length 23ft 9in (7.25m); width 12ft 3in (4.27m); height 10ft 1in (3.27m).
Weight: 153,000lbs (69,400kg).
Ground Pressure: 15.2lb/in² (1.07kg/cm²).
Power to weight ratio: 8.78hp/ton.
Engine: Maybach HL 230 P 30 V-12 water-cooled inline petrol engine developing 600bhp at 3,000rpm.
Performance: Road speed 24mph (38km/h); cross-country speed 11mph (17km/h); range 68 miles (110km); vertical obstacle 2ft 9in (0.85m); trench 8ft 2in (2.5m); fording depth 5ft 3in (1.6m); gradient 35 degrees.
History: In service with the German Army from 1944 to 1945.

The Tiger I had hardly entered service before the German general staff requested a bigger and better successor, superior in armour and hitting power to anything that the Soviet Army was likely to produce. Once again Porsche and Henschel were asked for designs which were to incorporate the latest sloped armour and the longer 71-calibre 8.8cm gun. Porsche updated its Tiger I design and this time was so sure of an order that it started work on the turret and actually put casting in hand. Unfortunately the Porsche ideas of electric transmission were once more rejected, supplies of copper being too small, and the contract went to Henschel for the second time. However, 50 Porsche turrets were made and fitted to the first models. Henschel then fitted its own turret, which was simpler and had better protection. Another requirement of the specification was to liaise with MAN in order to standardise as many parts as possible with the Panther II, which never appeared, and the

Below: The PzKpfw Tiger II with Henschel turret which was easier to build and also offered better protection than the Porsche turret fitted to the first 50 Tiger II tanks.

subsequent delays meant that production did not get under way until December 1943.

The Tiger II, known to its own side as the *Königstiger* and to the Allies as the Royal Tiger, was a massive and formidable vehicle. It was intended to dominate the battlefield, and that it could do, providing that its crew used it sensibly. It was the heaviest, best protected and most powerfully armed tank to go into production during World War II, and its armour and gun would do justice to a main battle tank today. The price paid for all this superiority was size, weight and low performance. Manoeuvrability, ground pressure and that subtle thing 'agility' all suffered, and inevitably the reliability of the over-stressed engine and transmission decreased.

The hull was welded, as was that of the Tiger I, but the armour was better sloped, using the experience of the T-34. Hull layout was similar to that of the Panther, and the large turret was roomy although the gun came right back to the rear wall and made a complete partition longitudinally. Some 80 rounds of ammunition were stowed round the turret sides and floor and there were plenty of racks and shelves for the minor equipment. The commander's cupola allowed an excellent view, though he usually chose to have his head out of the top. The long and powerful 8.8cm gun could outrange and out-shoot the main armament of nearly all Allied tanks, and this allowed the Tiger II to stand off and engage targets as it chose. Barrel wear was a difficulty with this high-velocity gun, and the later models had a two-piece barrel which allowed the faster-wearing part to be changed easily.

Only one model was built, and altogether no more than 485 examples were completed. Production never suffered despite the heaviest Allied bombing, and Henschel always had at least 60 vehicles in construction on its shop floors at any one time. At the peak it was taking only 14 days to complete a Tiger II. Severe fuel shortages forced the factory to use bottled gas for testing, though petrol was supplied for operations.

The Tiger II was introduced into service in the autumn of 1944, on the same distribution as the Tiger I, and again in small units of four or five. Its enormous size and weight made it a ponderous vehicle, often difficult to conceal; in a fast moving battle it was quickly left behind, and this fate did occur to several in Russia. But when used properly it was enormously effective and could engage many times its own numbers of enemy, and knock them all out without damage to itself.

Below: The PzKpfw Tiger II, or Royal Tiger as it was often called, fitted with Porsche-built turret for its 88mm KwK 43 L/71 gun, for which 80 rounds of APCBC and HE were carried.

GREAT BRITAIN

Having started the whole idea of armoured warfare, Britain proved to be remarkably slow to develop it to its logical conclusion. Between the two World Wars Britain did carry out trials with a formation known as the Experimental Mechanised Force in which armour, infantry, artillery, engineers and even aircraft were used together for the first time, but these ideas were not carried through. Generally, conservatism in tactical thinking, reflecting the trench warfare attitude, was probably more evident in Britain at this time than in any other country.

The conclusions drawn from these trials, and the well-founded advice of Liddell Hart, failed to be heeded so that, like the French, the British Army were supremely equipped in 1939 to fight the battles of 1919. The British entered World War II maintaining their insistence on three different types of tank, as if there was to be some curious social class in armoured warfare. Light tanks were used for reconnaissance, their armour and weapons too light for anything else, and were soon shown up to be little better than cannon fodder. The next, the cruiser, was intended as a fast, wide-ranging armoured cavalry horse, but armour had to be sacrificed to keep the weight down in order to achieve the required speed and performance. As with all British tanks the cruisers were under-engined and under-gunned, and this told heavily against them in the long-range desert battles where the German tanks could outshoot them with ease. The cruisers were meant to engage other tanks, and

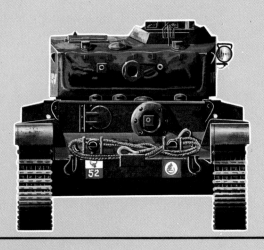

that was right: the tragedy was that they were never given the equipment with which to do it properly. The third class of tank was the infantry tank, a slow-moving, heavily armoured vehicle armed mainly, or often even solely, with machine-guns: a throw-back to World War I with a vengeance. It was intended to move with a walking infantry advance and engage enemy machine-gun nests or strong-points. The heavy armour was to give protection against light anti-tank fire and the vehicle was never intended to get into actual combat with another tank. The result was a series of tanks that were more or less invulnerable to small guns, but which were so pitifully armed as to be all but incapable of inflicting damage on their opponent's tanks, and with gross under-powering and almost total inability to manoeuvre against the more agile German vehicles. The exception was the A12 Matilda II, which had greatly increased armour, a three-man turret and 2pounder gun, and this tank gave a good account of itself in the early battles in the Western Desert.

Despite the lessons of pre-war experiments, the British Army never learned to use their armoured formations as separate shock troops. Luckily for the British, large numbers of American tanks became available from 1941; first Grants and later Shermans, which equipped many British armoured regiments from then on. Without these (despite the determination of the men) the North African battles would have had quite a different outcome.

A11 Matilda I Infantry Tank

Country of origin: Great Britain.
Crew: 2.
Armament: One .3in or .5in Vickers machine-gun.
Armour: 60mm (2.36in) maximum; 10mm (0.39in) minimum.
Dimensions: Length 15ft 11in (4.85m); width 7ft 6in (2.28m); height 6ft 1½in (1.86m).
Weight: Combat 24,640lbs (11,161kg).
Engine: Ford eight-cylinder petrol engine developing 70bhp at 3,500rpm.
Performance: Road speed 8mph (12.8km/h); range 80 miles (128km); vertical obstacle 2ft 1in (0.635m); trench 7ft (2.133m).
History: Served with the British Army only between 1938 and 1940.

The origin of the Matilda I lay in a request from General Sir Hugh Elles to Vickers for a tank to be built down to a price. Sir John Carden led the design team and the result was probably the most unfortunate one of his career. The concept of the infantry tank called for good protection, low speed to keep pace with infantry assaulting on foot, and only limited offensive power. It was thought to be sufficient to give the tank an armament of machine-guns and no more. These limits were bad enough, but the price limit was equally daunting at £6,000 for the complete vehicle. Not surprisingly the Matilda I was reduced to the barest essentials, and perpetuated a number of mistakes which had already been well aired.

The first was the crew. Two-man tanks had been shown to be scarcely workable in the 1920s and early 30s, but Carden was forced to return to a one-man turret because he could not afford the space for two. One machine-gun made a mock of the whole idea of fire-power, and to have a complete tank to carry one gun was a great waste of manufacturing effort and money. Finally, to give the vehicle a top speed scarcely better than that of a running man was quite ludicrous. Those were the limitations, however, and the General Staff accepted the design and the first production order was placed in April 1937. The first models were delivered in 1938 and issued to the 1st Army Tank Brigade, who took them to France in 1939. By 1940 139 had been built and they formed the greater part of the vehicle strength of the 1st Brigade. Their severe limitations showed up with frightening clarity

in the *Blitzkrieg*, and all were finally lost on the way to, or at, Dunkirk. Their crews fought valiantly, and they had one small success, but the tank was hopeless in battle.

Carden had built the smallest vehicle that he reasonably could and used as many existing components as possible. Since protection was important he put thick armour on the front and used a cast turret. The armour was more than satisfactory and was comfortably invulnerable to the German anti-tank guns in France. The suspension was a less happy story. It was the same as had been fitted to the Vickers 6ton (6,096kg) tank of 1928, and it could only cope with low speeds and moderate power outputs when carrying twice the weight it was designed for. The final drawback lay in the engine, which was the well-proved but low-powered Ford V-8. In order to drive the Matilda it had to be well geared down and the power was taken through a simple transmission to a rear sprocket. When the armament limitations became clear the turret was up-gunned by fitting the Vickers 0.5in machine-gun. This was some improvement, but it took more space in the small turret, and was tiring to use.

Above: An A11 Matilda I infantry tank. Clearly seen is the single smoke-bomb discharger mounted on the side of the turret. The frontal armour was almost impenetrable by any anti-tank gun of the time, but the vehicle had many faults which made it ineffective and expensive. A total of 139 were completed by August 1940 after which time the tank was relegated to training.

Left: Main drawback of the Matilda I was that it was armed only with a .303 Vickers machine gun operated by the commander/gunner. This was later replaced by a .50 machine gun, but when this was installed the turret became even more cramped.

Cruiser Tank Mark IV

Mks IV, IVA and VC; A13MkII
Country of origin: Great Britain.
Crew: 4.
Armament: One 2pounder gun and one Vickers 0.303 machine-gun (Mark IVA mounted a 7.92mm BESA).
Armour: 6mm (0.24in) minimum; 38mm (1.5in) maximum.
Dimensions: Length 19ft 9in (6.02m); width 8ft 4in (2.54m); height 8ft 6in (2.59m).
Weight: 33,040lbs (14,987kg).
Engine: Nuffield Liberty V-12 water-cooled petrol engine developing 340bhp.
Performance: Speed 30mph (48km/h); range 90 miles (144km); vertical obstacle 2ft (0.61m); trench 7ft 6in (2.29m); gradient 60 per cent.

Below: A Cruiser Mk IV, officially designated the A13 Mk II. This tank was developed from an American Christie tank purchased in 1936 and entered production in 1938. It was issued to the 1st and 7th Armoured Divisions by 1940.

History: Deliveries began in December 1938 and were completed in late 1939. Some 335 tanks were made and were issued to units of 1st Armoured Division in France in 1939/40. Some also went to the Western Desert where they were used by the 7th Armoured Division. Withdrawn from service during 1942.

The Cruiser Mark IV derived directly from a Christie tank bought in the USA in 1936. Morris Motors were given the task of redesigning the Christie to make it battle-worthy, and to do this they had to build a new hull and a better turret. The Christie could reach 50mph (80km/h) on roads, and very high speeds across country, but these had to be reduced since it was quickly found that the crew were injured by being thrown about.

The only engine available which gave the necessary power was the American Liberty aero-engine of World War I, and this was de-rated to 340hp to improve torque and reliability. The later Mark IVA had a Wilson combined speed change and steering gearbox and a BESA rather than Vickers coaxial machine-gun. The Mk IV CS was the close support model. The Christie suspension was a great success and gave the Cruiser a very good performance in the desert. It was retained on all British cruiser tanks for the rest of the war.

The turret had undercut sides and sloped upper plates, but the hull was still much of a box and had many sharp angles in which shot could lodge. Some extra plates were added to the desert Cruisers, but they were always under-armoured and after a short while in service various mechanical weaknesses became apparent and reliability was not as good as it should have been. Despite the shortcomings of the Cruiser it was a step forward for British tank design and it set the pattern for the later wartime cruisers.

Left: Cruiser Tank Mk IV of 1st Armoured Division in 1940. This particular tank has been fitted with additional armour plate over the mantlet. A total of 655 were built by Nuffield, LMS, Leyland and English Electric. The tank was essentially an up-armoured version of the earlier Mark II. Some were fitted with a 3.7in mortar for use in the close support role.

Below: Cruiser Mk IVA was the designation given to later production vehicles which had the Vickers .303 co-axial machine gun replaced by the 7.92mm BESA weapon, and additional armour.

A9 Mark I Cruiser Tank

Country of origin: Great Britain.
Crew: 6.
Armament: One 2pounder gun; three .303 Vickers machine-guns. (CS version had one 3.7in howitzer in place of the 2pounder.)
Armour: 14mm (0.55in) maximum; 6mm (0.25in) minimum.
Dimensions: Length 19ft (5.79m); width 8ft 2in (2.49m); height 8ft 8in (2.64m).
Weight: Combat 28,728lbs (13,013kg).
Engine: AEC Type 179 six-cylinder water-cooled inline petrol engine developing 150bhp.
Performance: Road speed 25mph (40km/h); cross-country speed 15mph (24km/h); range 150 miles (240km); vertical obstacle 3ft (0.92m); trench 8ft (2.43m).
History: Used by the British Army between 1938 and 1941.

The main British tank strength throughout the 1920s and the first half of the 1930s was made from the Vickers Medium Mark II, with the scouting (or reconnaissance) role being undertaken by light tanks of various kinds, ultimately types coming after the Carden-Loyd models. This combination was becoming out of date by 1934, quite plainly, and new designs were needed. In particular, it was becoming apparent to the General Staff that better medium tanks were required for the tank-to-tank confrontations which it was foreseen might occur on future battlefields. 1934 was not a good time to be planning major expenditure on military equipment, however; the depression was at its height, and money was almost unobtainable.

Sir John Carden set to work in 1934 to design a tank to meet a General Staff specification for a successor to the Vickers mediums, but with a slightly

Right: The A9 Mark I cruiser tank was designed by Sir John Carden from 1934, the first prototype being built in 1936. In 1937 125 were ordered, 50 from Vickers and 75 from Harland and Wolff.

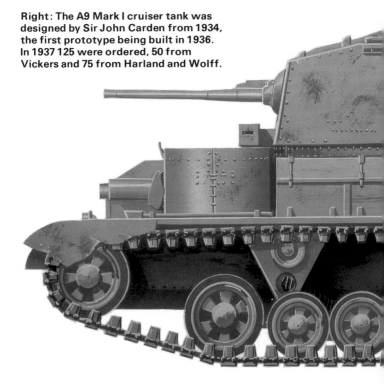

different role to fulfil. The difficulty with the tank specifications of the 1930s was that nobody had any clear idea what they wanted the vehicles to do in the next war. The old ideas of crossing trenches had not entirely died out, yet it was realised that tanks would be needed to act on their own, much in the way that cavalry had done, and also there was a need for armoured reconnaissance. The result of this somewhat baffled thinking was to stipulate a family of three types: cruisers, which were meant to be the cavalry type of machine, yet able to fight it out with other tanks if called upon to do so; infantry tanks which moved at slow speed with the assaulting infantry, and only had to knock out machine-gun nests (a throwback to 1918); and light tanks for the reconnaissance role. Nobody thought out the armament require- ▶

Above: Main armament of the A9 was a turret mounted 2pounder gun with a .303 Vickers MG coaxial to the right. Each side of the driver was a turret armed with a single .303 MG. A few A9s were built for the close support role; these had their 2pounders replaced by a 3.7 inch howitzer. The A-9 was the first British tank to have a power-operated turret and an auxiliary engine.

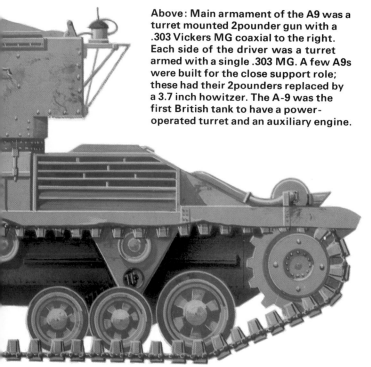

Above: A9 Mark I from front clearly showing position of .303 hull machine gun turrets.

Right: The A9 was followed by the A10 Mark II cruiser with increased armour but no hull machine gun turrets. A total of 175 A10 cruisers were completed by late 1940.

ment to cope with these different tasks, and the cruisers were particularly badly served since they were given either the 3pounder, which was feeble, or the later 2pounder, which had good armour penetration for its day, but could not fire HE shells. All medium tanks were well supplied with machine-guns, which were quite useless against other armoured vehicles.

With these crippling restrictions around him Sir John Carden produced the first A9 early in 1936. It epitomised all that had served to restrict the design. It was lighter than the mediums so that it could be powered by a commercial engine. At the same time it tried to incorporate all the best features of the Medium Mark III, and to a great extent succeeded, but only by making everything so much lighter that the armour protection was largely negated. The overall weight was only two-thirds that of the Medium Mark III, and the design weight was even less than this. The general layout was reasonable for its day, with a central turret, engine at the rear and acceptable cross-country performance from the suspension. One of the features which spoiled the A9 was the vertical armour, all of it too thin, and the multitude of angles and corners in which armour-piercing shot could lodge, instead of being glanced off.

A point in the A9's favour, however, was the fact that it was the first British tank to have power (hydraulic) traverse for the turret. This was a substantial step forward, and was to be followed on all succeeding designs. Another notable first was the carriage of an auxiliary engine for starting, battery charging, and driving a fan for the fighting compartment. These were sensible innovations, and went some way to offsetting the failings of the A9 as a fighting tank. The crew was a generous allowance of six men, split into a commander, gunner, loader, driver and two hull machine-gunners. The driving and fighting compartments were combined into one, hence the need for a fan to clear the fumes from three machine-guns and a 3pounder. The two hull machine-guns were mounted in small sub-turrets in front, one on each side of the driver. The gunners were cramped, and so was the driver, and the whole concept was strongly reminiscent of World War I. The arcs of

fire of the machine-guns were limited, and their use was therefore doubtful.

The engine was originally meant to be the Rolls-Royce car engine from the Phantom series. The pilot model, however, showed that the vehicle was under-powered and an AEC bus engine was substituted. This just managed to give the tank a speed of 25mph (40km/h) on the road, but had to be geared down considerably to do it. The suspension could manage the cross-country speed of 15mph (24km/h) but the pilot model at first shed its tracks at these speeds. Trials started in 1936 and at the same time the War Office was changing its policy on tanks generally.

The A9 had begun as a medium tank replacement, but now the cruiser idea was born, and the vehicle became the Cruiser Tank Mark I. The first contract for a limited number was placed in August 1937 with Vickers, which was to build 50. Another contract with Harland and Wolff of Belfast specified a further 75, and these constituted the total production. The limitations of the design were soon obvious and the A13 was put in hand as the next model. The intrinsic limitations of the 2pounder meant that tanks could not deal with strongpoints or pillboxes, and this brought about the concept of the Close Support tank. CS tanks carried large-calibre guns for firing HE and other types of ammunition, and a few CS models of the A9, mounting a short-barrelled 3.7in howitzer, were built. The three machine-guns remained. The suspension was a Vickers refinement of the popular multi-bogie system, and it was successful enough to be incorporated into the later Valentine almost without alteration. The steering brakes were mounted externally on the rear sprockets, where they cooled easily, but were perhaps a little exposed to damage. The tracks were narrow, and none too strong, but the low power output of the engine and the relatively gentle gearbox gave them a reasonably long life.

A9s were issued to 1st Armoured Division, which took them to France in 1939 and 1940, and left practically all of them at Dunkirk. The 2nd and 7th Armoured Divisions took the type to Egypt and used it until 1941, by when it was clearly well out of date and out-gunned.

A12 Matilda II Infantry Tank

Matilda II Marks I to V.
Country of origin: Great Britain.
Crew: 4.
Armament: One 2pounder gun; one .303in Vickers machine-gun (Mark I); one 2pounder gun; one 7.92mm BESA machine-gun (Mark II); one 3in howitzer; one 7.92mm BESA machine-gun (Mark II CS).
Armour: 0.55in (14mm) minimum; 3in (78mm) maximum.
Dimensions: Length 18ft 5in (5.61m); width 8ft 6in (2.59m); height 8ft 3in (2.51m).
Weight: 59,360lbs (26,926kg).
Power to weight ratio: 7.17hp/ton (Mark III).
Engine: Two AEC six-cylinder inline diesels developing a total of 174bhp (Marks I and II); two Leyland six-cylinder inline diesels developing a total of 190bhp (Mark III).
Performance: Road speed 15mph (24km/h); cross-country speed 8mph (12.8km/h); range 160 miles (256km); vertical obstacle 2ft (0.61m); trench 7ft (2.13m); fording depth 3ft (0.91m).
History: Served with the British Army from 1939 to 1945. Also used by Australia and Russia.

When the Matilda I was still in the prototype stage the War Office was already debating whether it could be up-armoured and up-gunned to meet a revised General Staff specification which said in effect that if tanks were to survive while supporting infantry on foot they must be able to withstand the fire of anti-tank guns, yet carry sufficiently heavy armament to cope with enemy infantry, gun positions and tanks. This brought about a fundamental change in approach to the design of infantry tanks. Previously it had been considered that machine-guns were sufficient armament, but the new specification required some sort of shell-firing gun, and a large enough turret in which to put it. At first it was thought that Matilda I (A11) could be given a two-man turret and a 2pounder gun, but it was soon apparent that there was no hope of this within the narrow hull limits, and in any case the weight of the turret would have defeated the already overloaded Ford engine and another would

have to be fitted. The weight of the tank was intended to be kept down to 14 tons (14,225kg), and the A11 could not possibly meet it with the changes already mentioned, so a new design was called for.

This new tank was entrusted to the Design Department at Woolwich Arsenal and was largely based on the prototype A7 of 1932. The same suspension was used, suitably strengthened, and the same powerplant of twin commercial diesels was put in. The requirement for thick armour meant that a cast turret and bow plate would be the most satisfactory solution, but British industry in the mid-1930s had only a very limited capacity for large castings, and this severely restricted the firms who could be given contracts for this work. It also meant that riveted and welded hulls and turrets were retained on British tanks long after other countries had gone over to castings. However, the contract for Matilda II was given to the Vulcan Foundry of Warrington in November 1936 and they produced a wooden mock-up by ▶

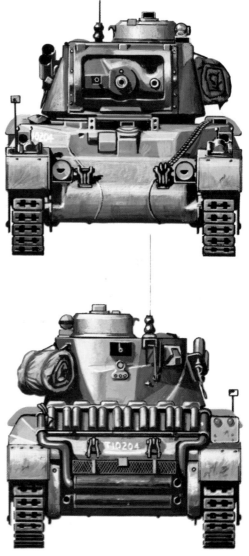

Right and below: A12 Matilda II infantry tank which entered service in 1939 and was first used by the 7th Royal Tank Regiment during the retreat to Dunkirk. Just under 3,000 Matilda IIs were built before production stopped in August 1943. The Matilda formed a major part of the British armoured forces during the 8th Army's battles in the Western Desert.

Left: The Matilda II was last used as a gun tank in North Africa during the battle of Alamein in July 1942. After this date it was used for special roles such as clearing mines. The Australian Army continued to use the Matilda in the Far East and also developed more specialised models for their own use including a 'dozer and a flamethrower. The latter was called the Frog and was followed by the Matilda Murray.

Above: The Matilda III was the close support model and had the 2pounder gun replaced by a 3inch howitzer. It was powered by two Leyland 95hp diesels instead of two 87hp AEC diesels.

Right: Matilda Baron III mine clearing vehicle. The flail was powered by two Bedford engines mounted in boxes at the hull rear.

April 1937. Another year elapsed before the pilot model (made in mild steel) was ready, the delay mainly being occasioned by difficulties in the supply of the Wilson gearbox. Trials with this model were carried out during 1938, but an initial order for 65 tanks was given even before the pilot model appeared, and shortly afterwards this was increased by a further 100. Luckily the trials showed the design to be satisfactory, the only changes being minor ones to the suspension and engine cooling.

Re-armament started in earnest during 1938 and tanks were in desperately short supply, so further orders were given, which were more than Vulcan could manage. Other firms were called in, and contracts were let to Fowler, Ruston & Hornsby, LMS Railway Works, Harland & Wolff and North British Locomotive Works. Vulcan were the main contractor, and undertook most of the casting work. The Matilda was not easy to put into mass production, mainly because of the castings, and certain features of the design were quite difficult. For some reason the side skirts were in one piece, involving another large casting, and an immediate easement to production was to reduce the number of mud chutes from six to five. By September 1939 only two Matildas were in service, but by the spring of 1940 at least one battalion (7th Royal Tank Regiment) was equipped and the tank gave a good account of itself in the retreat to Dunkirk and the subsequent fighting around the port. At the same time several units in Egypt had received it, and used it in the early campaigns against the Italians.

After Dunkirk the Matilda I was dropped altogether and the Matilda II became the Matilda, by which name it was known for the rest of the war. In Libya in 1940 and 1941 the Matilda was virtually immune to any anti-tank gun or tank that the Italians could deploy. This happy state of affairs continued until about mid-1941 when the first units of the *Afrika Korps* appeared and brought their 8.8cm *Flak* guns into action in the ground role against tanks. This gun could knock out the Matilda at ranges far beyond the 2pounder's ability to reply, and the Matilda began to fade from the battle. Attempts to up-gun it to carry a 6pounder were failures because the turret ring was too small to take a larger gun, and the last action when Matilda was used as a gun tank was the first battle of El Alamein in July 1942.

The Matilda was a conventional British tank with the usual three compartments in the hull, the driver sitting centrally behind the nose plate. There was no hull gun, an unusual departure for the time, but sensible, for they were rarely effective in battle. The heavy cast turret was small, and the three men in it were cramped. In the CS version with a 3in howitzer, space was even scarcer. The commander had a circular cupola, but it gave him only limited vision and this lack of good vision was the worst feature of the vehicle, though it was no worse than many other designs of that time. The

turret was rotated by hydraulic power, and was one of the first to use this system developed by the Frazer Nash Company, who also developed the turret controls for aircraft. Some 67 rounds of 2pounder and 4,000 of .303in ammunition were carried. The twin AEC diesels were coupled together and drove to a Wilson epicyclic gearbox and a rear sprocket. The suspension was derived from the A7 and was either known as the 'scissors' or 'Japanese' type. It originated with the Vickers Medium C, though a similar type also appeared on the French tanks of the 1920s and 1930s. It consisted of sets of bogies linked together and working against horizontal compression springs. Each bogie had four rollers, arranged in pairs so that to each suspension point there were four pairs of rollers, two link units, and two springs; the whole was supported by one vertical bracket attached to the hull. On each side there were two of these complete units, one four-roller unit and one large road wheel at the front. The track ran back along return rollers at the top of the side skirt. This apparently complicated arrangement worked well, though it inevitably limited the top speed. Mark III Matildas, and later marks, were fitted with Leyland diesels which gave slightly more power and were made in larger numbers than the AECs. The Mark V fitted an air servo on top of the gearbox to ease gear changing, but apart from these minor modifications, the Matilda stayed very much as it had been designed.

Up to the first battle of El Alamein the Matilda had gained the somewhat high-blown title of 'Queen of the Battlefield', or at least some people called it that. After El Alamein it was apparent that the type was well past its best, and it was replaced by the increasing quantities of Grants and Shermans. The problem was to know what to do with the Matildas, most of which were still in good running order. The thick armour and reasonable protection made it an attractive vehicle for special applications, and it was the first British tank to be equipped as a flail mine-clearer, some of which were used at El Alamein. The flail was followed by a host of other devices, including anti-mine rollers, large demolition charges, bridge-layers, dozer blades, Canal Defence Lights (CDL) to illuminate the battlefield at night, gap-crossing devices and flamethrowers. One was even used as an experimental radio-controlled vehicle. Matildas were supplied to the Australian Army, which used them in the Pacific campaign and still had it in service for driver training as late as 1953. The Australians paid particular attention to developing flamethrowing variants which were useful against Japanese infantry positions in the jungle, and a dozer version was also frequently used in that theatre, mainly to improve tracks for wheeled vehicles to follow the tanks. Some Matildas went to Russia, where the thickness of armour was admired, but as in the Churchill later on, the 2pounder gun was politely dismissed as near useless. There are also some reports that the suspension clogged in the winter snow, though the Russians were not particularly communicative about the equipment provided to them.

After four or five years continuous use the Matildas were worn out, and it was not worth rebuilding them. A few were still in service at the end of the war, though not as gun tanks. However, the Matilda can claim to be the only British tank which served right through World War II and there are very few others which can approach that record, whatever their nationality.

Crusader Cruiser Tank

Crusaders I to III
Country of origin: Great Britain.
Crew: 5 in the Mark I; 4 or 5 in the Mark II; 3 in the Mark III.
Armament: Crusader I one 2pounder gun and two 7.92mm BESA machine-guns; Crusader II one 2pounder gun and one or two 7.92mm BESA machine-guns; Crusader III one 6pounder gun and one 7.92mm BESA machine-gun.
Armour: Crusader I 40mm (1.57in) maximum and 7mm (0.28in) minimum; Crusader II 49mm (1.93in) maximum and 7mm (0.28in) minimum; Crusader III 51mm (2in) maximum and 7mm (0.28in) minimum.
Dimensions: Length 19ft 8in (5.99m); width 8ft 8in (2.64m); height 7ft 4in (2.23m).
Weight: Combat Crusader I and II 42,560lbs (19,279kg); Crusader III 44,240lbs (20,040kg).
Ground Pressure: 14.7lb/in^2 (1.04kg/cm^2).
Engine: Nuffield Liberty 12-cylinder water-cooled inline petrol engine developing 340bhp.
Performance: Road speed 27mph (43.2km/h); range 100 miles (160km); vertical obstacle 2ft 3in (0.685m); trench 8ft 6in (2.59m); gradient 60 per cent.
History: In service with the British Army from 1939 to 1943.

The Crusader was to a great extent developed from the Covenanter, which it outwardly resembled. The Covenanter was a pre-war design which started in 1937 and was similar to the Cruiser Mark IV, or A13. The Crusader followed in the design pattern of these cruisers, but was designated to be a heavy cruiser, which was a difficult specification to fulfil within the weight and size limitations. It was equally difficult to fulfil when the main armament was only a 2pounder gun. The specification did show, however, that the limitations of the previous models had been appreciated. They were too lightly armoured, but were also too lightly armed, and nothing could be done about this in 1939.

The Crusader was built by a consortium of firms under the leadership of Nuffield Mechanisations Ltd, and 5,300 were made before production ceased. The hull was similar to that of the Covenanter, with a long flat deck and a well raked glacis plate. The Christie suspension was very similar, except for an extra wheel station and the spring units, which were contained inside the hull. This suspension was the strong point of the Crusader and enabled

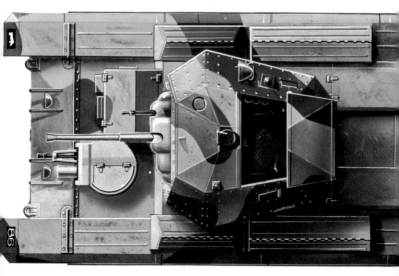

it to move much faster than the official top speed of 27mph (43.2km/h). In the Western Desert Crusader drivers and fitters opened up the engine governors to let the Liberty engine go as fast as it could, and the result was sometimes a speed as high as 40mph (64km/h). The Christie wheels could cope with this quite well and still give the crew a tolerable ride, the casualty usually being the engine. The hull was divided into the usual three compartments, with the driver sharing the front one with a hull machine-gunner in the first two marks. The Crusaders I and II had a 7.92mm BESA machine-gun mounted in a small auxiliary turret on the left front deck. This turret was subsequently removed, and omitted from later marks, thus allowing more space for storage, particularly of ammunition. The fighting compartment had the turret above it, and was none too large. It was not ideal for the commander either since he had to combine the tasks of commanding, gun loading, and often wireless operating as well: the usual drawbacks to a two-man turret. The engine was the elderly but well tried Nuffield Liberty, basically an aero-engine from World War I de-rated from 400 to 340hp. The early Crusaders had considerable trouble with their engines, mainly from the cooling arrangements. The large fan often broke its drive shafts, and the aircleaners were difficult to ▶

Right and below: The Crusader I (Cruiser MkVI) as it appeared in North Africa with the 9th (Queen's Royal) Lancers, 1st Armoured Division. Plagued by mechanical failure and weak armour, Crusaders nevertheless served in all the major North African campaigns. There were 5,300 built but they were out-dated and were generally withdrawn by 1943. A few versions served on in Italy.

keep clean, but after some experience and modification the engine went very well.

Undoubtedly the tank was rushed into service before all its development troubles had been ironed out, and in its first engagement in June 1941, Operation 'Battleaxe', more Crusaders fell into enemy hands through mechanical failure than through battle damage. Nevertheless the tank went on to fight in all the major actions throughout the Desert Campaign, and by Alamein the Crusader III with a 6pounder gun had arrived. The 6pounder required a larger mantlet, which was flatter than that for the 2pounder and rather ugly. The same mantlet could also be fitted with a 3in Close Support howitzer, though not many were so modified. The Crusader was outdated by the end of the North African campaign. A few went to Italy and some hulls fought in North-West Europe adapted to such uses as AA vehicles and gun-towers. In the desert the Crusader became popular, and its speed was liked, but the armour was too thin, and the armament always too weak.

Right: Crusader (Cruiser Tank Mk VI) advance during the North African campaign. The driver's hatches are in the open position and the 7.62mm turret-mounted BESA MG has been removed.

Below: The final production version of the Crusader was the Mk III of which 144 were built between May and July 1942. This model has a 6pounder in place of the standard 2pounder gun and increased armour protection. Variants of the Crusader included command tanks, gun tractors, 'dozers, ARVs, mine clearing tanks and various anti-aircraft tanks. The latter were armed with a 40mm gun, twin 20mm or triple 20mm Oerlikon cannon.

Valentine Infantry Tank Mark III

Marks I–XI.
Country of origin: Great Britain.
Crew: 3 (4 in Mks III and IV).
Armament: One 2pdr and one 7.92mm BESA machine-gun (Mks I–VII); one 6pdr and one 7.92mm BESA machine-gun (Mks VIII–X); and one 75mm gun and one 7.92mm BESA machine-gun (Mk XI).
Armour: 8mm (0.31in) minimum; 65mm (2.56in) maximum.
Dimensions: Length (overall) 17ft 9in (5.41m); width 8ft 7½in (2.63m); height 7ft 5½in (2.27m).
Weight: 35,840lb (16,257kg).
Engine: AEC petrol engine developing 135hp (Mk I); AEC diesel developing 131hp (Mks II, III, VIII); GM diesel developing 138hp (Mks IV, IX); and GM diesel developing 165hp (Mks X, XI).
Performance: Road speed 15mph (24km/h); range 90 miles (144km); vertical obstacle 3ft (0.91m); trench 7ft 9in (2.36m); gradient 60 per cent.
History: Entered service with the British Army in May 1940; obsolete by May 1945. Also used by Canada, France and the Soviet Union. Also built in Canada.

The Valentine tank was a private venture by Vickers-Armstrong Ltd and built to the prewar concept of the British Army that there should be two types of tank, a cruiser for the open warfare as practised by cavalry, and a heavy support tank for the infantry. These latter were required to be heavily armoured and performance was a secondary consideration. In designing the Valentine, however, Vickers took several mechanical components from existing cruisers which they were building for the War Office, and so saved both time and effort in trials and production. In fact, the Valentine was more of a well armoured cruiser than a pure infantry tank, but its low speed was always a handicap to its use in open warfare.

The name of Valentine derived from the date when the design was submitted to the War Office, 14 February 1938. An order was not placed until July 1939, when 275 were demanded in the shortest possible time. The

first ones were issued to service in May 1940 and several were given to the cavalry to make up for the losses of the Dunkirk evacuation and only later found their way to the tank brigades for their proper role of infantry support. By the time production ceased in early 1944 8,275 Valentines of all marks had been built. Some 1,420 were made in Canada and 1,390 of these, together with 1,300 from UK, were sent to Soviet Russia. The Russians put them into action straight away and admired the simplicity and reliability of the engine and transmission, but they disliked the small gun which was of little use on the Eastern Front. In some cases they replaced it with their own 76.2mm tank gun.

In British service the Valentine first saw action in the Western Desert in 1941 and successive marks of it continued in the desert right through until the end of the campaign. Some were also landed with the 1st Army in Tunisia. These desert Valentines gained a great reputation for reliability and it is reported that after El Alamein some motored over 3,000 miles (4,830km) on their own tracks following the 8th Army. A squadron was landed with the assault force on Madagascar in 1942 and the 3rd New Zealand Division had Valentines in the Pacific campaign. Some of these tanks had their 2pdr guns replaced by 3in howitzers for close support work. A very small number went to Burma and were used in the Arakan, and a few were put into Gibraltar. By 1944, when the invasion of North-West Europe was mounted, the Valentine had been superseded as a gun tank, but the hull and chassis had already been utilised in a wide variety of different roles, and in these guises many Valentines were taken to France.

Probably no other tank has had so many changes built on to the basic structure. In addition to going through 11 marks as a gun tank, the Valentine was converted for DD drive (amphibious), bridgelaying, flamethrowing and more than one type of minefield clearing. It was an invaluable experimental vehicle for all manner of strange ideas: in one case a stripped chassis was fitted with rockets in an attempt to create that Jules Verne concept – the flying tank. It failed spectacularly.

As with most tanks the hull was divided into three compartments, driving, fighting and engine. The driver sat on the centre line of the vehicle and was rather cramped. He got in and out by a hatch above his head, and when closed down his vision was restricted to a small visor and two episcopes.

The fighting compartment had the turret mounted on it, and the turret was the worst feature of the whole tank. It was always too small, no matter which ▶

Left: Valentine I of A Squadron, 17/21st Lancers, 6th Armoured Division, in 1941. A total of 8,275 were built in Britain. Another 1,420 were built in Canada, all but 30 of which were supplied to Russia under Lend-Lease.

Left: Valentine tank captured by the Germans in North Africa and subsequently used by the Afrika Corps, only to be knocked out by its original owners in a latter battle. Both the Germans and the British made considerable use of captured vehicles in campaigns in North Africa to supplement their own vehicles.

Left: Valentine II of 50th Royal Tank Regiment. This tank was similar to the Mk I but had an AEC 131hp diesel in place of the AEC 135hp petrol engine. Valentine IIs used in North Africa were fitted with sand shields each side and a jettisonable long range fuel tank at the rear.

Left: Valentine XI used as a command vehicle in 30 Corps Anti-tank Regiment, Royal Artillery, in North-West Europe during 1944/45. The Valentine XI had improved (but still poor) armour protection and a 75mm gun in place of the 6pounder of the Valentine X, and a 165hp General Motors diesel engine.

mark is considered, and no amount of redesign ever cured this trouble. In the marks which had a three-man crew the two in the turret were overworked, or at least the commander was. He had to load the main armament, command the vehicle, select targets for the gunner, and operate the wireless. His vision was extremely restricted because there was no cupola for him and he had to rely on a single episcope when closed down. This naturally meant that he rarely did close down properly, and left his hatch open so that he could bob up to get a view. This led to casualties as soon as the fighting started. In the back of the turret was the No 19 radio set, which also had a short range set built into it for infantry co-operation. The commander operated these two sets, and also gave instructions to his crew through an RT set. Not surprisingly the Marks III and V, with a four-man crew, were popular with commanders, though the space in the turret was no better and the vision just as bad.

The gun was as poor as the turret. The 2pdr was an accurate little weapon but it was already outdated in 1938 though it survived in the early desert battles because it could just defeat the Italian and lighter German tanks at its maximum range. However, 1,000 yards (915m) was the most that it could do and another drawback was the lack of an HE shell for general targets. Some 79 rounds were carried, and about 2,000 rounds for the coaxial BESA. The Marks VIII, IX and X were fitted with a 6pdr though even that was nearly out of date by the time it appeared and, incredibly, the Marks VIII and IX had no coaxial machine-gun with their 6pdr, so the crew were quite incapable of engaging infantry except with the main armament. The Mark X had the BESA installed, but this cut down the space left for the crew. Most marks carried a Bren LMG inside the turret and this gun could be mounted on the roof, though of course it could only be fired by the commander fully exposing himself through his hatch. The Canadian-built Valentines were equipped with Browning 0.3in machine-guns in place of the BESA and some, but not all, of the later marks were fitted with smoke dischargers on the turret sides.

The turret was traversed with a hydraulic motor controlled by a spade grip. This gave a good lay, but the final touches were done by handwheel. With the 2pdr the gun's elevation was laid by the gunner's shoulder-piece, there being no gearing involved at all. The later guns were laid in elevation by a hand gear wheel.

In contrast with the fighting compartment, the engine was well housed and easy to get at. Maintenance was easy for a tank, and the entire unit was most reliable. The Mark I had the AEC petrol engine, but all successive marks used diesels, which appear to have given little trouble. The power went through a five-speed Meadows gearbox to steering clutches and steering brakes, the latter being prominently mounted on the outside of the drive sprockets.

All the marks were built with riveted plate armour and virtually no curves anywhere. Canadian Valentines and some of the British-built Marks X and XI were given cast nose plates which were both stronger and cheaper than the built-up versions, but in general the armour layout was uninspired. The maximum thickness of 65mm (2.56in) was naturally in front, but at the rear and on top it was down to 8mm (0.31 in) and by 1944 this was too thin.

The suspension was typical of its period and is usually described as being a slow-motion type. It consisted of two three-wheeled bogies on each side, the wheels being sprung by horizontal coils in linked bogies. The front and rear wheels were bigger than the others, giving a distinctive appearance to the side view, and the hull was carried well above ground level. The track was returned on three top rollers and was built up from cast track links. These worked very well in all conditions except the Russian winter, when apparently they collected packed snow and stopped the tank altogether.

The Valentine DD version was used mainly for training, but a few were landed during the Italian campaign. None went to Normandy. The basic Valentine was carefully waterproofed and fitted with a collapsible screen which suspended the hull below water level. An external screw was fitted and this had to be hinged up when the vehicle beached.

Below: Bishop was a Valentine II tank fitted with new open-topped turret armed with 25pounder gun. The first 100 were ordered in 1941 from Birmingham Carriage and Wagon Company.

A22 Churchill Infantry Tank

Churchills I to VIII.
Country of origin: Great Britain.
Crew: 5.
Armament: Churchill I one 2pounder gun, one 7.92mm BESA machine-gun and one 3in howitzer in the hull; Churchill II one 2pounder gun and two 7.92mm BESA machine-guns; Churchill III–IV one 6pounder gun and two 7.92mm BESA machine-guns; Churchill IV NA 75 one 75mm gun, one .3in Browning machine-gun and one 7.92mm BESA machine-gun; Churchill V and VIII one 95mm howitzer and two 7.92mm BESA machine-guns; Churchill VI and VII one 75mm gun and two 7.92mm BESA machine-guns; Churchill I CS two 3in howitzers and one 7.92mm BESA machine-gun.
Armour: Churchill I–VI 102mm (4in) maximum and 16mm (0.63in) minimum; Churchill VII and VIII 152mm (6in) maximum and 25mm (1in) minimum.
Dimensions: Length 24ft 5in (7.44m); width 10ft 8in (3.25m); height 8ft 2in (2.49m).
Weight: Combat Churchill III 87,360lbs (39,574kg).
Engine: Two 6-cylinder Bedford water-cooled inline developing 350bhp.
Performance: Road speed 15.5mph (24.8km/h); cross-country speed 8mph (12.8km/h); range 90 miles (144km); vertical obstacle 2ft 6in (0.812m); trench 10ft (3.048m).
History: In service with the British Army from 1941 to 1952. Also used by Eire, India and Jordan.

The Churchill was the replacement for the Matilda II, the specification having been drawn up with that in mind. It was to the project number A20 that the new tank was first assigned, and design work started in September 1939 by Harland and Wolff of Belfast. The A20 went as far as four prototypes in June 1940, but no farther. It was to have been rather like a World War I rhomboidal, with side sponsons mounting 2pounder guns. Vauxhall Motors took over the contract for the next infantry tank, the A22, and were able to use the A20 as a starting base. The beginnings were not auspicious with Dunkirk just over, and virtually no armour force in the UK at all. Vauxhall were given one year in which to design, test and produce the tank, the stipulation being that the production lines had to be assembling the type within 12 months. With this extraordinary time limit to constrain them, the design team set to work and the first pilot model was actually running within seven months. The first 14

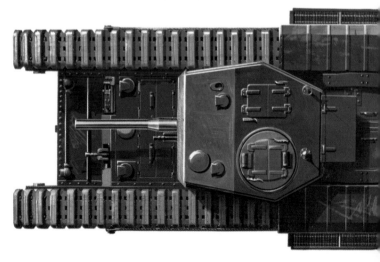

production tanks were off the line by June 1941, within 11 months of design starting, and volume production followed on quickly after that.

Such a rush was bound to bring its problems, and the early marks of Churchill had no lack of them. The engine was a purpose-built 'twin six', not unlike two Bedford lorry engines laid on their sides and joined to a common crankcase. The idea was to make an engine that was both compact and accessible. Compact it certainly was, but it was scarcely accessible. The petrol pump was driven by a flexible shaft underneath the engine, and had an unfortunate habit of snapping. The hydraulic tappets, copied from American engines, were meant to run without adjustment, but frequently broke, necessitating a change of engine. The carburettor controls were also hydraulic, and also got out of adjustment. The power output was low for the weight of the hull, and the overall response sluggish. In fact the tank was rushed into service before it was ready. After a year of use most of the troubles were ironed out and it became quite reliable, but the first 12 months saw it gain a reputation for fragility and unreliability which it never completely lived down. The A22 specification was more modern than any that had gone before, and it called for a low silhouette and thick armour, both requirements for survival on the battlefield.

Unfortunately the first Vauxhall design perpetuated the worst features of the armament stagnation that had blighted British tanks since 1918. The ▶

Right and below: A Churchill III armed with a 6pounder gun, co-axial 7.92mm BESA MG and another 7.92mm BESA mounted in the hull. The Churchill was used in action for the first time during the Dieppe landing in August 1942 when a number of Mk I and II tanks were used fitted with wading equipment. 5,600 Churchills were built.

Above: Churchill armed with 6pounder gun. The tank gave a very good account of itself in the mountainous terrain of Tunisia.

Above right: A post-war view of a Churchill AVRE Mk VII (FV 3903) which was armed with a 165mm breech loaded low velocity gun and is shown here carrying a 10-ton fascine which it would drop into anti-tank ditches and other obstacles.

Right: Churchill AVRE with deep wading equipment and Standard Box Girder bridge attachment at the front of the hull during the D-Day landings, in the background is a Sherman flail tank.

turret carried only a 2pounder gun, and by 1940 it was becoming clear that this size was a complete anachronism. The difficulty was that there was none other. The 6pounder design was in being, but the Ordnance Factories were tooled up for 2pounders, and in the desperate days after Dunkirk there was no time to change over, so 2pounders it had to be for another year or more. A 3in Close Support howitzer was mounted low down in the front of the hull, alongside the driver. This was much like the arrangement in the French Char B, and there was little enough faith in that idea; but again, the designers had little option but to use the weapons available to them. A very few Close Support Churchills I were built, and these had the unusual armament of two 3in howitzers, the second one replacing the 2pounder gun in the turret, but the idea was not pursued further. The Churchill II and later marks dropped the hull gun in favour of a BESA machine-gun. By March 1942 the 6pounder was available and was fitted to the turret of the Churchill III in that month. Improvement followed and the Mark VII had a 75mm gun, the Mark VIII a 95mm Close Support howitzer, and some North African Mark IVs were re-worked in Egypt to accommodate a 75mm gun and 0.3in Browning machine-gun in the turret, both these weapons being taken from Shermans and perhaps Grants.

The armour of the Churchill was probably the best part of the vehicle, and was very heavy for the time. The thickness of the frontal plates went up with successive marks, and most of the earlier marks were re-worked, as time and

supplies permitted, to be given extra 'appliqué' plates welded on. Turrets increased in size and complexity and the Mark VII was given the first commander's cupola in a British tank to have all-round vision when closed down — a great step forward, though it was common enough in German tanks by that time. The hull was roomy, which was fortunate in view of the amount of development which was done on it, and the ammunition stowage was particularly generous. The Mark I was able to carry 150 rounds of 2pounder and 58 of 3in howitzer ammunition, still leaving room for five men. The hull was sufficiently wide to allow the Mark III's 6pounder turret to be fitted without too much trouble, though the 75mm and 95mm weapons caused a little difficulty and had a rather smaller turret-ring than was ideal. These latter turrets looked a little slab-sided, as a result of the fact that some were built up with welding, rather than cast as complete units.

The Churchill was the first British tank with the Merritt-Brown regenerative steering, which had been tried out in the A6 10 years before. This system not only saved a great deal of power when turning, but also enabled the driver to make much sharper turns, until in neutral he could turn the tank on its own axis. This system, or some variant of it, is now universally used by all tank designers. Another innovation, for British AFVs at least, was the use of hydraulics in the steering and clutch controls, so that driving was far less tiring than it had been on previous designs, and the driver could exercise finer judgement in his use of the controls. The suspension was by 11 small road wheels on each side. ▶

Each of these wheels, or more properly bogies, was sprung separately on vertical coil springs, and the amount of movement was limited so that the ride was fairly harsh. However, such a system had the merits of simplicity, cheapness, and relative invulnerability to damage; each side could tolerate the loss of several bogies and still support the chassis, and the manufacture and fitting of bogies was not too difficult.

Churchills were used on most of the European battlefronts. The first time they were in action was the Dieppe raid of August 1942, in which several Mark Is and IIs took part, together with a few Mark IIIs. Few got over the harbour wall, and most were either drowned when disembarking, or captured. A number of Mark I, II and III examples were sent to Russia, and a few Mark IIIs were tried at Alamein. Thereafter they were used in Tunisia and Italy in ever-increasing numbers until the end of the war. Several brigades of Churchills were deployed in North-West Europe, where their thick armour proved very useful, but throughout the campaign the Churchill was hampered by being outgunned by German armour.

There were many variants on the Churchill chassis as it was quickly found that it was well suited to such tasks as bridging, mineclearing, armoured recovery, and (probably best of all) flamethrowing. The Churchill was also a

particularly successful Armoured Vehicle Royal Engineers (AVRE) and fulfilled several different RE roles until replaced by the Centurion AVRE in the early 1960s. Altogether 5,460 Churchills were produced, and they remained in service in varying numbers until the 1950s. The lack of adequate gun power was realised quite early in the Churchill's life, however, and in 1943 Vauxhall developed an improved version carrying a 17 pounder in the turret. The turret-ring had to be enlarged, and so the hull was widened. The armour remained the same thickness, and weight went up to 50 tons — 112,000lbs (50,736kg). To support this extra load the tracks were widened, new bogies fitted, and the Bedford engine geared down. Top speed was only 11mph (17.6km/h) and although the prototypes were still being tried in 1945, the idea came to nothing, and the Black Prince, as it was to have been called, was scrapped.

Below: Following trials with a flamethrower installed in a Valentine tank in 1942 it was decided the following year to instal the system in a Churchill, with the fuel being carried in a trailer towed behind the tank. This became known as the Churchill Crocodile and entered very successful service in 1944.

A27M Cromwell Infantry Tank

Cromwell Marks I to VIII.
Country of origin: Great Britain.
Crew: 5.
Armament: One 6pounder gun; one 7.92mm BESA machine-gun co-axial with main armament; one 7.92mm BESA machine-gun in hull (Marks I to III); one 75mm QF Mark V or VA gun; two 7.92mm machine-guns (Marks IV, V and VII); one 95mm howitzer; two 7.92mm BESA machine-guns (Marks VI and VIII).
Armour: 0.31in (8mm) minimum; 3in (76mm) maximum; 0.4in (10mm) minimum; 3in (76mm) maximum in welded variants; 4in (102mm) appliqué armour.
Dimensions: Length 20ft 10in (6.35m); width 10ft (3.04m); height 9ft 3¾in (2.84m).
Weight: 61,600lbs (27,942kg).
Ground Pressure: 14.7lb/in² (1kg/cm²).
Power to weight ratio: 21.8hp/ton.
Engine: Rolls-Royce Meteor V-12 water-cooled petrol engine developing 600bhp at 2,250rpm.
Performance: Road speed 40mph (64km/h); cross-country speed 18mph (29km/h); range 173 miles (277km); vertical obstacle 3ft (0.92m); trench 7ft 6in (2.28m).
History: Served with the British Army from 1942 to 1950.

The Cromwell emerged from a General Staff specification drawn up in late 1940 and early 1941 for a 'heavy cruiser'. The cruisers built to the traditional ideas of a light fast vehicle capable of fulfilling the cavalry role of pursuit and exploitation had proved to be unequal to the modern battlefield in two vital areas, protection and gun power. The 1941 specification called for cruiser tanks with an all-up weight of around 25 tons (25,401kg), front armour of 2.75in (70mm) thickness, and a 6pounder gun on a 60in (1.52m) turret ring. Nuffield produced the first model, designated the A24 and originally called the Cromwell. This was an improved Crusader and used several of its components, among which was the Liberty engine which quickly proved itself incapable of performing satisfactorily in a tank weighing nearly 60,000lbs (27,216kg). The name was soon changed to Cavalier, and the unsuccessful vehicle was used only for training and a few specialist roles.

Early in 1941 Leyland had collaborated with Rolls-Royce in looking for a satisfactory tank engine, and hit upon the Meteor, a de-rated Merlin aircraft engine. With 600hp this gave more than enough power for the heavy cruiser tanks, and since the main components were already well developed it seemed likely that it would be both robust and reliable. Leyland therefore began work

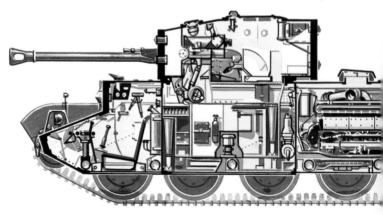

on a tank which came to be called the Centaur, but this was really a Cromwell with a Liberty engine. There were no Meteors to be had when the Centaur was first produced, so it was fitted with the available Liberty engines, and was a bit more successful than the unfortunate Cavalier. A particular feature was the fact that the engine compartment could accept the Meteor when it became available, and many of the production run were so converted after 1943. Meanwhile the Birmingham Railway Carriage and Wagon Company had taken on the design of the final version of Cromwell and produced the first pilot version in January 1942. At this date the name was still causing confusion, and it was variously known as the A27M (M for Meteor), Cromwell M, or Cromwell III. The nomenclature was only finally cleared up when Cavalier and Centaur were confirmed as names. Because of the failures from too few trials, the Cromwell was exhaustively tested, a luxury at that time of the war, and the first production models did not appear until January 1943; which was far too long. The Meteor engine gave little trouble, and amply demonstrated that power was a necessary feature of tank design. The first engines were built by Rolls-Royce themselves in order to get the design right, but production was switched away from them as soon as possible, to leave them free to concentrate on aircraft engines, and the Meteor was put out to contract.

Just as the first Cromwells appeared, the General Staff changed its policy towards tank armament. Up till then the main armament gun had been required to be used in an anti-tank role, but experience in the desert and North Africa showed that after a breakthrough the main targets were not tanks at all, but dug-in infantry and anti-tank guns. What was needed was ▶

Right and below: Front and rear views of Cromwell IV cruiser. Frontal insignia are, from left to right, the unit number, the squadron number, and sign of the Guards Armoured Division.

Below left: Cutaway side view of Cromwell IV with 75mm QF Mk V gun and co-axial 7.92mm BESA MG.

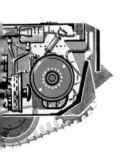

not an AP-firing gun but one that could fire a substantial HE shell against these softer targets. The Shermans and Grants carried a 75mm gun with such a performance and there was a demand for these to be mounted on British vehicles. The new General Staff specification reflected this approach, though it was also agreed that the need for a Close Support (CS) tank had not yet vanished. The fitting of a 75mm gun inserted some further delay into the programme, and there was also a need to retrofit 75mm guns into tanks that had been produced with the 6pounder. The first 75mm guns were delivered in late 1943, and by this time they were probably already close to the end of their time, though they had to be used until the end of the war. The 75mm was a new gun, developed from the 6pounder and using several components from that gun. The barrel was the same, bored out and shortened and fitted with a muzzle brake. The breech mechanism was also similar, and not surprisingly there were several initial defects, not fully overcome until May

Right: A Cromwell Mk III, formerly known as Centaur or Cromwell X, powered by Rolls-Royce Meteor engine. A total of 64 rounds of ammunition were carried for the 6pounder gun. To increase the operational range an auxiliary fuel tank was fitted at the rear.

1944. The ammunition was American, taken from Lease-Lend supplies without modification, and gave no trouble. The American gun was interesting in that it had been directly derived from the French 75mm (*soixante-quinze*) of World War I. In 1933 these 75s were adapted for tank use by fitting a sliding breech and different buffer and recuperator, but the ammunition was still the same original French design, and indeed French ammunition could be fired. After Syria was taken from the Vichy French in late 1941, a quantity of French field gun ammunition was shipped to the Western Desert and used in Grant tanks. The gunner used a normal telescope for sighting the 75mm, but he could also use a range drum and clinometer for long range shooting. The two BESA machine-guns were mounted in the turret and hull, the latter displaying the last surviving remnant of the idea of mounting machine-guns all round the hull, which went back to the first tanks of World War I. Later on in the war many Cromwell crews were sceptical of the value of the hull gun, and it was frequently left out on the variants.

The hull conformed to the standard British design of three compartments, and was built of single armour plate, either welded or riveted. In the front compartment were the driver and hull gunner, separated from the turret by a bulkhead with an access hole in it. The commander, gunner and loader were in the turret in the centre compartment, contained in a rotating basket, the gunner on the left with the commander behind him and the loader on the right. The turret traversed by hydraulic power and was extremely accurate in fine laying. The turret could be fully rotated through 360 degrees in 15 seconds. The commander had a cupola, the early models having only two episcopes, the later ones with eight, thereby providing all-round vision. Twenty-three rounds of 75mm ammunition were stowed ready for use in the turret and the balance of a full load of 64 rounds was stowed around the walls of the compartment. Some 4,950 rounds of BESA ammunition were carried. The No 19 wireless set was in the back of the turret behind the

Above: Canadian-crewed Cromwell tanks in action in France in 1944. In the armoured regiments the Cromwells were usually employed with Sherman Fireflies (Sherman armed with the potent 17pounder gun), in the troop ratio of three Cromwells to one Firefly. Close support models had a 95mm howitzer. Generally outgunned by the heavier German tanks, the Cromwell squadrons nevertheless succeeded with speed and manoevrability.

loader, who listened in on the net. In the rear compartment the engine was placed between two fuel tanks and two large air cleaners. The radiators were right at the back, mounted upright. Transmission was through a Merritt-Brown regenerative gearbox, which had proved successful in the Churchill tank in 1941. It was used in a cruiser for the first time in the Cromwell, but the combination of Meteor and Merritt-Brown was to be the mainstay of British tank designers for years to come. The suspension was Christie-type, adapted from the A13 and strengthened. Even so it could not tolerate the top speed of 40mph (64km/h) and after the Mark IV the maximum speed was reduced to 32mph (52km/h) by gearing down the final drive. The track was wider than that of the A13, and the ride that it gave was remarkably good.

The Cromwell proved itself to be both fast and agile, and was popular with its crews. Maintenance was not too difficult, and the reliability of the Meteor was a blessing to those who had had to cope with the vagaries of overstrained Liberty engines in other designs. A possible drawback for the crew was the difficulty of getting out in a hurry, especially for the driver and hull gunner. Later marks were given side doors to the front compartment so that the two men could climb out whatever the position of the turret and gun. In allowing for these doors some stowage space was lost on the track guards, and there was only a small bin behind the turret. Local enterprise often fitted extra bins, for space was tight for five men. Cromwells were used for training throughout ▶

1943 and early 1944, and the opportunity for action did not come until the Normandy invasion. It was then the main equipment of the 7th Armoured Division and a number of armoured reconnaissance regiments. After the breakout from Caen, the Cromwell was able to do the job it was designed for, and exploit the assault. Supported by 95mm Howitzer CS versions the Cromwell squadrons out-manoeuvred and outran the heavier German tanks, but they were always outgunned, even by the comparatively light Panthers. Attempts to fit the 17pounder gun were a failure, and the Cromwell crews relied for their success on superior training and manoeuvrability when in action. The attempt to fit the 17pounder gun resulted in a tank called the Challenger, built to the specification A30. The first model appeared in August 1942, based on a lengthened Cromwell with an extra wheel station. Performance was poor because the hull was too narrow for the large turret, and the extra weight and longer track base reduced speed and agility. Nevertheless it was approved for service early in 1943 and 260 were built. A

Above: Cromwell VII armed with 75mm gun; this was a Cromwell re-worked with applique armour welded onto the hull front, wider tracks, stronger suspension and reduced final drive ratio.

later attempt to improve on the Challenger produced the Avenger, a Challenger with a better turret, but only thin sheet steel on the roof.

The final step in trying to make Cromwell into an SP gun was in 1950, when the Centurion 20pounder was put into a two-man turret on the normal Cromwell hull. This just about worked, and it was issued to the Territorial Army and sold in small numbers to Austria and Jordan. As a gun tank Cromwell was numerically the most important British cruiser of the war, and though never the main battle tank of the army, it supplemented the Shermans in all British tank formations by 1945. Its speed and power were the best ever seen in British tanks till that time, and there was plenty of scope for development in the basic design.

A34 Comet Cruiser Tank

Country of origin: Great Britain.
Crew: 5.
Armament: One 77mm gun; one 7.92mm BESA machine-gun co-axial with main armament; one 7.92mm BESA machine-gun.
Armour: 102mm (4in) maximum; 14mm (0.55in) minimum.
Dimensions: Length 25ft 1$\frac{1}{2}$in (7.66m); width 10ft (3.04m); height 8ft 9$\frac{1}{2}$in (2.98m).
Weight: Combat 78,800lbs (35,696kg).
Ground pressure: 13.85lb/in^2 (0.88kg/cm^2).
Engine: Rolls-Royce Meteor Mark 3 V-12 water-cooled petrol engine developing 600bhp at 2,550rpm.
Performance: Road speed 32mph (51km/h); range 123 miles (196km); vertical obstacle 3ft (0.92m); trench 8ft (2.43m); gradient 35 per cent.
History: In service with the British Army from 1944 to 1958. Still used by Burma and South Africa.

The requirement for the Comet was first seen during the tank battles in the Western Desert in late 1941 and early 1942, when it was apparent that British tanks had no gun capable of defeating the Germans. The Cromwell, whilst an excellent tank, had been given too small a gun, which could not fire HE. Nor was its 6pounder very powerful against armour. An attempt to upgun it to carry the 17pounder met with little success (the Challenger), and by late 1943 there was an urgent need for a fast cruiser with reasonable protection and a gun capable of taking on the later marks of German tank.

Leyland was given the task of developing the new tank early in 1943, the first priority being to decide upon a suitable gun. The criterion chosen was to look for the most powerful gun that could be mounted on Cromwell, and then a tank would be built using as many Cromwell components as possible. After much searching and deliberation Vickers-Armstrong designed a lighter and more compact version of the 17pounder, the Vickers HV 75mm. This gun fired the same shell as the 17pounder but used a shorter and wider cartridge case which was easier to handle in a turret. It was slightly less powerful, and had a shorter barrel and lower muzzle velocity, but it was still far ahead of any gun carried on Allied AFVs at that time, except the SP tank destroyers. To

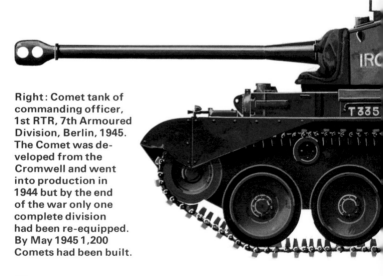

Right: Comet tank of commanding officer, 1st RTR, 7th Armoured Division, Berlin, 1945. The Comet was developed from the Cromwell and went into production in 1944 but by the end of the war only one complete division had been re-equipped. By May 1945 1,200 Comets had been built.

avoid confusion in names and ammunition supply, the new gun was called the 77mm.

The first mock-up of the Comet was ready in late September 1943, and production was planned to be under way in mid-1944. The need for the Comet had become pressing. The first prototypes were delivered early in 1944, but there was a good deal of redesign to be done, and what had started as an up-gunned Cromwell soon reached the point where 60 per cent of the vehicle was a complete redesign, albeit a similar design. The hull was largely untouched, and there was criticism of the retention of the hull gun and the ▶

Above: Comet cruiser tank showing 77mm high velocity gun and bow-mounted 7.92mm BESA machine gun during closing stages of the war. Infantry are riding on deck and track guards.

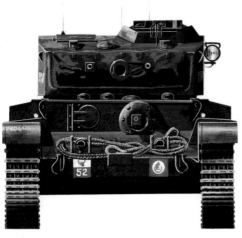

Above: Front view of a Comet cruiser tank showing position of the hull-mounted 7.92mm BESA machine gun.

Right: The Comet was designed under the parentage of Leyland Motors Limited as the A34 cruiser tank. Main armament consisted of an Ordnance Quick Firing 77mm Mk 2 which in fact had a calibre of 76.2mm but was called the 77mm to avoid confusion with the 17 pounder gun. This fired an APCBC projectile weighing 7.7kg which would penetrate 109mm of armour at a range of 457 metres, it could also fire a high explosive round. The Comet tank is still in operational service with both Burma and South Africa in 1981!

vertical front plate it required. The Cromwell's belly armour was also kept, although this had been shown to be too light. But there was no time to do more, and despite front line pressures continual changes and modifications meant that the first production models were not delivered until September 1944, and did not reach the first units until just before Christmas. The 11th Armoured Division was re-equipped with Comets in the first months of 1945, and was the only division to have a complete stock by the end of the war. Other divisions were issued with Comets as the year went by, though more slowly. In early 1949 the Centurion replaced the Comet, although Comets were still in Berlin and Hong Kong until the late 1950s.

Although practically a new tank, the Comet was easily recognisable as a Cromwell successor, and it was in essence an up-gunned and up-armoured version. The hull was welded, with side doors at the front for the driver and hull gunner. The turret was also welded, with a cast mantlet and front armour. The space inside was good, and access was fairly easy. The commander was given all-round vision with the same cupola as the Cromwell, and ammunition was stowed in armoured bins, a distinct step forward. The turret was electrically traversed, a development of the excellent system tried out in the Churchill, and to provide adequate electricity a generator was driven by the main engine. As with the later marks of the Cromwell, there were only two stowage bins over the tracks, and there was a prominent bin at the back of the turret. This to some extent counter-balanced the overhang of the gun. The suspension was meant to be identical with that of the Cromwell, but it was quickly found that this was not adequate for the extra weight and so it was

strengthened and given return rollers. With this suspension the Comet was remarkably agile and tough, and its cross-country speed could often be more than the crew could tolerate with comfort. The Meteor engine had adequate power for all needs and on a cross-country training course a good driver could handle a Comet like a sports car — and frequently did. It was sufficiently strong to stand up impressively to high jumps at full speed.

The Comet only went to one variant on its solitary mark, surely a record for any British tank: the main feature of the variant was a change in the exhaust cowls, a modification found necessary after the Normandy fighting. These helped to hide the tank at night, and as also at that time it was usual to lift infantry into battle on the decks and track guards, the cowls protected them from the exhaust.

The Comet was the last of the cruisers, and also the last properly developed British tank to take part in the war. It was not universally popular, and met strong criticism at first, mainly because its detractors believed that it perpetuated the faults of the Cromwell, which in some minor respects it did. This was particularly so in the case of the nose plates and the hull gun. However, to remove them would have involved an extensive redesign and the building of new jigs for the factory. This was out of the question in 1943. The disappointment at the lack of effective belly armour is less easy to refute, since it should have been foreseen, but it was only appreciated too late. Perhaps most of the exasperation of the users sprang from the fact that it was such a good tank and came so late that it was never given a chance to prove itself properly.

SOVIET UNION

Although Russia took an early interest in armoured cars it was not until the capture in 1919 of two Renault FT light tanks that they became interested in tanks. A modified version of the Renault was put into production as the KS in 1920. From then on tank design, development and production proceeded rapidly in the Soviet Union, and it is estimated that between 1928 and 1937 some 21,000 of all types had been built.

Tactics had not been neglected either and, quite naturally, since French influence had always been strong in Russia, the first armoured units were modelled on the French ones, being thereby tied to infantry formations in a purely supporting role. However, some of the thinking of the Germans probably filtered through with the mutual cooperation arrangements of the 1920s and 1930s. The first mechanised brigade was formed in 1929/30 with the first mechanised corps following in 1932. But between then and the German invasion of Russia in 1941 there were many reorganisations, most of the tanks being attached to the infantry rather than being used in their designed role of breakthrough and exploitation. Many army officers were removed from their posts and executed, to be replaced by new officers with little experience in armour.

However, the experiments with the mechanised corps were used as the basis for the armoured formations which fought through World War II, and from them also was deduced the primary lesson of all armoured warfare, that

firepower counts above all other considerations.

As with most other armies, the Russians had three types of tank – light, medium and heavy. Losses in the first few months of the war were enormous, but even at this time the Russians had already designed and put into production two new tanks that were to turn the tide from the following year – the T-34 medium and the KV-1, both of which were accepted for service on December 19, 1939; within two years, German tanks were to meet their match in these.

The T-34, in its various guises, formed the backbone of Soviet tank units. Owing much to the American M1931 Christie design, it had the right combination of armour, mobility and firepower. It was, and still is, and object lesson in good design, and its appearance was a revelation to the German Army. At first its effectiveness was to some extent reduced by the then current Soviet habit of using tanks in cavalry charges. A mass of armoured vehicles was made to rush a position in the same way as a cavalry squadron, and it was some time before it was discovered that it was often more profitable to deploy bigger-gunned tanks, stand off and shell the opposition into submission.

When the Germans invaded, many of the tank manufacturing plants were moved eastwards to the Urals, but production was maintained and was soon increased. In 1941 the Russians built 6,500 tanks; in 1942 25,000 armoured fighting vehicles were built and by the end of the war over 100,000 tanks and self-propelled guns had been produced.

T-28 Medium Tank

T-28, T-28 06 1938, T-28 06 1940, T-28*M*, IT-28 and T-29-5.
Country of origin: Soviet Union.
Crew: 6.
Armament: One 76.2mm gun; three DT machine-guns.
Armour: 20mm to 80mm (0.79in to 3.15in) depending on model.
Dimensions: Length 24ft 5in (7.44m); width 9ft 3in (2.82m); height 9ft 3in (2.82m).
Weight: 61,729lbs (28,000kg) to 70,547lbs (32,000kg) depending on model.
Ground pressure: 10.25lb/in^2 (0.73kg/cm^2) to 10.95lb/in^2 (0.78kg/cm^2) depending on model.
Power to weight ratio: 18.1hp/ton to 15.9hp/ton depending on model.
Engine: One M-17L 12-cylinder water-cooled petrol engine developing 500hp at 1,450rpm.
Performance: Road speed 23mph (37km/h); range 140 miles (220km); vertical obstacle 3ft 5in (1.04m); trench 9ft 6in (2.9m); gradient 80 per cent.
History: Served with the Russian Army from 1933 to 1941.

Work on building a suitable type of medium tank was undertaken during the early 1930s. After trials with numerous prototypes in this tank class (including the T12, T24 and TG), which for a multiplicity of reasons proved unsuitable for mass production, in 1932 the Leningrad Kirov plant built a new prototype medium tank based on the general design of the British A6E1 16 ton (16,257kg) tank. A specimen of this vehicle was not purchased (being still secret at the time), but it is believed that much information was obtained on it through espionage.

The first Soviet specification for a multi-turreted 16 ton medium tank, intended for breaking through strongly fortified defensive zones and for exploitation by mechanised brigades, was issued to the Kirov plant in 1931. The specification demanded a crew of five men, 20mm to 30mm (0.79in to 1.18in) armour, a 500hp engine and a maximum speed of 37mph (60km/h). The armament was to comprise one 45mm gun and a machine-gun in the main turret, and one machine-gun in each of the two forward subsidiary turrets. Some 7,938 rounds of machine-gun ammunition were to be carried. A prototype, which weighed 17.3 tons (17,575kg), was completed during 1932. After trials with the prototype vehicle, it was

requested that heavier armour be applied and that the main armament be increased to 76.2mm (with 70 rounds).

A specification was then laid down for a 27.56 ton (28,000kg) medium tank, designated T-28. The final model was accepted for adoption by the Red Army on 11 August 1933. All tanks of this type were provided with two-way radio equipment, having the characteristic frame aerial around the top of the main turret. They were also fitted with smoke-emitters. In later production vehicles a device was employed to stabilise the main turret. Designed by A. A. Prokofiev, this greatly improved accuracy of fire while on the move. The T-28 was noted for its quiet, smooth motion and abnormal capability for crossing trenches and other terrain obstacles. During 1938 this tank was subjected to extreme modification (now called T-28 06 1938). The existing armament (16.5 calibres long) was replaced by the 76.2mm L-10 gun of 26 calibres length.

T-28 tanks were employed against the Japanese in 1939 and also during the Russo-Finnish War. In the course of this war, it was discovered that the armour was inadequate and, as the result, modification of the armour was carried out. This was achieved by 'screening' (*yekpanirovki*) suitable parts of the existing armour. The turret and hull frontal plates were increased from 50mm to 80mm (1.97in to 3.15in), the sides and rear to 40mm. Consequently, the weight of this new model (called T-28 06 1940 or T-28*M*) rose to 31.5 tons (32,000kg). Despite the increase in weight the speed was not significantly impaired. This up-armoured tank gained much acclaim during the break-through of the Mannerheim Line in 1940. Its mass production was terminated soon after the conclusion of hostilities between the USSR and Finland, when the type was replaced in production by the new T-34 medium tank.

The chassis of the T-28 was used for several types of experimental self-propelled gun as well as special-purpose tanks (eg bridgelayer IT-28 and a mine-clearing tank). During 1934 the design bureau at the Kirov Factory developed a wheel/track variant of the T-28, called the T-29-5. Although this never passed beyond the prototype stage, it formed the first link in the eventual development of the T-34.

Top of page: The T-28 was the first medium tank to enter service with the Soviet Army in 1933. Its design owed a lot to the British A6E1 16 ton tank which was designed by Vickers Armstrongs in the late 1920s but did not enter service with British Army.

Left: Prototype of the T-28 was completed in 1932 and following trials it was decided to increase both armour and firepower. The T-28 was used during the war against Finland, when again it was found to be under-armoured. It was improved with special plating and the tank then gave a good account of itself, despite the extra weight. The T-28 also served against Japan in 1939.

BT-7 Fast Tank

BT-7, BT-7A, BT-7M, BT-7U, BT-7TU and variants, plus BT-1, BT-S and BT-5.

Country of origin: Soviet Union.
Crew: 3.
Armament: One 45mm M1935 gun; one co-axial 7.62mm DT machine-gun. (Some vehicles had an additional 7.62mm DT machine-gun in turret rear and a P.40 machine-gun.)
Armour: 22mm (0.87in) maximum; 10mm (0.39in) minimum.
Dimensions: Length 18ft 7in (5.66m); width 7ft 6in (2.29m); height 7ft 11in (2.42m).
Weight: 30,644lbs (13,900kg).
Ground Pressure: 11.25lb/in² (0.79kg/cm²).
Power to weight ratio: 36hp/ton.
Engine: One Model M17T 12-cylinder water-cooled petrol engine developing 500hp at 1,650rpm.
Performance: Road speed on wheels 46mph (73km/h); road speed on tracks 33mph (53km/h); range on wheels 450 miles (730km); range on tracks 270 miles (430km); vertical obstacle 1ft 10in (0.55m); trench 6ft 7in (2m); gradient 60 per cent.
History: In service with the Russian Army from 1935 to 1945.

Next to the T-26 light infantry-accompanying tank, the *BT* fast tank was the most prolific AFV in the Red Army during the 1930s. The initials *BT* form an acronym for *Bistrokhodny Tank*, or Fast Tank. It was known among Soviet tankmen as the *Betka* (Beetle) or as the *Tri-Tankista* (Three Tanker — as the result of its three-man crew).

As distinct from most of the other Soviet vehicles at that time, which were based on British Vickers models, the *BT* tank was derived from an American design by J. W. Christie. This design was also later taken up by the British to develop their famous Cruiser tank range, the most famous member being the

Crusader. The basic Christie vehicle was purchased by Soviet officials in America during 1930 and one vehicle was shipped back to Russia during that year and delivered to the Kharkhov Locomotive Works. After extensive tests of the Christie vehicle, on 23 May 1931 the Revolutionary Military Council of the USSR authorised the tank for Red Army use and requested its mass production. The drawings for the *BT* tank prototype were delivered to the *Komintern* Factory in Kharkhov during August 1931.

On 3 September 1931, the first two prototypes, designated *BT*-1, left the factory gates and were delivered to the Red Army for trials. This first vehicle was provided with machine-gun armament only, and the Red Army test commission which investigated the tank requested that the production model ▶

Right: Front view of late model of BT-7 with conical turret and twin horn periscopes. The gun is a modification of the standard M-1935 firing an armour piercing round with a muzzle velocity of 820 metres a second. One of the features of the BT-7 was that its tracks could be removed, so enabling it to run at high speed on roads.

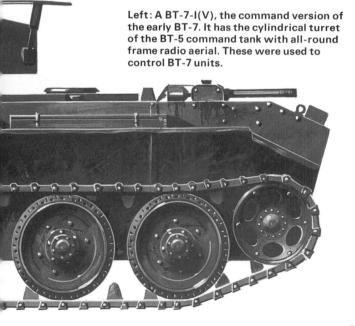

Left: A BT-7-I(V), the command version of the early BT-7. It has the cylindrical turret of the BT-5 command tank with all-round frame radio aerial. These were used to control BT-7 units.

be armed with an artillery weapon. In the meantime the *BT-2* model, still with machine-gun armament, was developed in limited quantities. After the production of a small number of vehicles, however, the *BT-2* tank received a 37mm Model 1930 tank gun mounted in the original machine-gun turret. During 1932 the Red Army requested that the *BT* tank be armed with a more powerful weapon, in the form of the 45mm gun. After various prototypes had been tested, the *BT-S* model was accepted. This mounted a 45mm gun in a turret almost identical to that fitted to the T-26 light tank. A co-axial 7.62mm DT machine-gun was also installed. Commanders' vehicles, which received the suffix *U* or *TU* (*BT-5U* or *BT-5TU*), were provided with two-way radio equipment, which was mounted in the turret overhang, thereby displacing some of the 45mm ammunition. As in the case of the T-26 commander's model, the turret was fitted with the characteristic frame aerial.

The *BT* tank was intended for large, independent long-range armoured and mechanised units (called *DD* groups). These were to act in the rear of enemy positions and take out nerve centres such as headquarters, supply bases, airfields, etc. Under such circumstances high speed was a great advantage. One of the basic attributes of the Christie design was the ability of the tank to run on either tracks or the road wheels. Track drive was used when moving across country or along poor roads, whilst wheel drive was used for long strategic road drives. The time taken to change from one mode to the other was put at between 10 and 15 minutes. This ability to run on wheels, however, was never actually exploited by the Red Army in military operations. When the tank was operated in the wheeled mode, the tracks were attached along the track guards, and engine power was transmitted to the rear pair of wheels. The two front road wheels could be turned to provide steering. In contrast to most other tanks, where two steering levers were employed, the *BT* was controlled by a steering wheel.

As the result of large-scale exercises carried out by the Red Army during the early 1930s, it was realised that the long-range *DD* groups required some form of accompanying artillery to provide artillery fire-support during the attack. For this reason, special artillery support tanks, which received the suffix *A*, were developed. The first of these, the *BT-5A*, was introduced in 1935. It mounted a short-barrelled 76.2mm gun in a turret very similar to that used as the main one on the T-28 medium tank. As a result of combat experience, the Red Army requested that the *BT* be redesigned with welded armour and that the armour be sloped to increase its immunity. Thus there

emerged the *BT-7* model, a vast improvement over the previous models. Ammunition stowage comprised 188 45mm rounds and 2,142 7.62mm rounds.

As in the case of the *BT-5*, a commander's model was developed, designated *BT-7U* or *BT-7TU*. The first series of this vehicle still retained the original cylindrical turret of the T-26 tank, however. In 1938, following experience against the Japanese in Manchuria, the new turret which had been designed for the T-26 light tank was also fitted to the *BT-7*. A commander's version of this model was also produced. To provide artillery fire-support the *BT-7A* version was developed. This had the same turret as the *BT-5A*. Other alterations to the *BT-7* were the use of a more powerful engine and an improved transmission system. During 1938 the new V-2 diesel engine had been developed specifically for tank use, and this was installed in all subsequent *BT-7* tanks. To distinguish it from previous models, the vehicle was designated *BT-7M*; it has, however, also been referred to as the *BT-8*. This new engine developed 500hp at 1,800rpm, and being a diesel power-plant allowed the *DD* groups a much greater range of operation than had been possible previously. It also reduced the fire risk, since diesel fuel is not so volatile as petrol.

Several specialised and experimental vehicles were developed from the *BT* tank. During 1936 the experimental *BT-IS* (investigator tank) was developed. This had heavily sloped armour that shrouded the tracks. This vehicle contributed greatly to the eventual development of the T-34 tank. During 1937 several *BT* tanks were equipped with schnorkels, enabling them to deepford water obstacles. Such vehicles were designated *BT-5PH*. As the *BT-5* and *BT-7* models gained numerical significance in the Red Army, the older *BT* models were used to develop special-purpose vehicles such as the *BT* bridgelayer, smoke tank and chemical tank.

Below left: BT-7 tanks accompany infantry in an attack on Japanese units in the Khalkin-Gol area of Manchuria/Mongolia in 1939. The Russians deployed 3 divisions and 5 armoured brigades, commanded by the General Zhukov (of WWII fame).

Below: Late production BT-7 tanks move through Gorky Street, Moscow, in November 1941. The BT-7 chassis was also used for specialised versions such as bridgelayer and smoke tank.

KV-1 Heavy Tank

KV-1, KV-1s, KV-2, KV-3 and KV-85.
Country of origin: Soviet Union.
Crew: 5.
Armament: One 76.2mm gun (various types); three 7.62mm DT machine-guns. (Some vehicles had an additional machine-gun in the turret rear and a P-40 AA machine-gun.)
Armour: 100mm (3.94in) to 75mm (2.95in), varying with model.
Dimensions: Length 20ft 7in (6.273m); width 10ft 2in (3.098m); height 7ft 11in (2.413m). (Dimensions varied slightly according to models.)
Weight: 104,719lbs (47,500kg), varying slightly with model.
Ground Pressure: 10.68lb/in² (0.75kg/cm²).
Power to weight ratio: 12.6hp/ton, varying with model.
Engine: One Model V-2-K 12-cylinder water-cooled diesel developing 600hp at 2,000rpm.
Performance: Road speed 22mph (35km/h); range 156 miles (250km), vertical obstacle 3ft 8in (1.2m); trench 8ft 6in (2.8m); gradient 70 per cent
History: Served with the Russian Army from 1940 to 1945.

At the outbreak of World War II, the Russian Army was practically the only armed force in the world to be equipped with production heavy tanks. The first of these, the KV-1 (Klim Voroshilov) was designed by a group of engineers at the Kirov Factory in Leningrad, under the direction of Zh. Kotin. Work began in February 1939 and the State Defence Committee approved a mock-up in April. The completed tank was demonstrated to the Red Army staff in September. It was accepted as standard at the same time as the T-34 medium, on 19 December 1939.

Production began in February 1940 and in that year 243 vehicles of the type were produced. A platoon of these, meanwhile, was sent to Finland for combat tests, and in February 1940 the tanks took part in the breakthrough of the Finnish main position. Not one of them was destroyed, although companion multi-turreted models were knocked out. Subsequent production was undertaken at the Chelyabinsk Tractor Factory to where in September 1941, as a result of the imminent German threat to Leningrad, the Kirov Factory was evacuated. By June 1941, however, when the Germans attacked, 636 had been built. In Chelyabinsk the Kirov Factory was amalgamated with the Chelyabinsk Tractor Factory, and other industry transferred there, to form the immense complex called 'Tankograd'. This became the sole Soviet industrial establishment producing heavy tanks and heavy self-propelled guns for the remainder of the war. By the time of the Battle of Moscow, 1,364 KVs had been built; of course, many of these had been destroyed or captured ▶

Above: KV-1 heavy tank production line at the Leningrad defence plant in October 1942. This plant worked throughout the 900 day siege. The KV-1 was designed at the Kirov factory under the direction of Kotin in February 1939 and was accepted for service in December 1939 with production commencing in 1940.

Right and below: A KV-1A heavy tank showing 7·62mm DT machine gun in the turret rear. The KV-1 was first used in action against Finland in 1940 and aquitted itself well. The 76·2mm gun of the KV-1 was the same as that fitted to the T-34/76.

Above: KV-1s built with funds donated by farmers in the Moscow area are presented to representatives of the Red Army by a group of patriotic donars. Such presentations were common among many countries during World War II.

Above right: A KV-2 heavy tank armed with a 152mm howitzer. It was first used by the Red Army against the Mannerheim line defence in 1940 during the Russo-Finnish War, but it had such poor performance that production was stopped.

Right: KV-1s, armed with the same 76mm gun as installed in the T-34/76 tank, on their way to the front at Leningrad in 1942.

in the meantime. Throughout the war, Tankograd supplied the Red Army with some 13,500 heavy tanks and self-propelled guns on this chassis.

Alongside the KV-1 tank, which was armed with the same gun as the T-34 (76mm), a special artillery fire-support version, the KV-2, was adopted. This had a massive box-shaped turret mounting a 152mm howitzer. Immediately after the start of production of the KV-1 and KV-2, the Kirov Factory received orders to design an even heavier tank with more powerful armament (107mm gun) and thicker armour. A prototype, designated KV-3, was built at the beginning of 1941 but the German attack interrupted plans for its mass production. During the period 1941—42, therefore, production of the KV-1 continued. The KV-2 was dropped as the result of its poor performance. Successive models of the KV-1 received thicker armour and some had castings in place of welded components. A new longer-barrelled gun was also introduced.

Experience at the front showed that the KV was now becoming too slow, so a lighter, faster version, the KV-1s, was introduced during the second half of 1942. As the need arose for more powerful armament, an 85mm gun was adopted in autumn 1943 for a model designated KV-85. In subsequent attempts to improve the KV tank a whole range of experimental vehicles was produced, but eventually the tank was replaced by the new IS (Iosef Stalin) series which was equipped with much better armament and also represented a radical approach to armour protection.

T-60 Light Tank

T-60 and T-60A
Country of origin: Soviet Union.
Crew: 2.
Armament: One 20mm ShVAK cannon; one 7.62mm DT machine-gun.
Armour: 7mm to 20mm (0.28in to 0.79in).
Dimensions: Length (overall) 14ft 1in (4.3m); width 8ft 1in (2.46m); height 6ft 2in (1.89m).
Weight: 11,354lbs (5,150kg).
Ground pressure: 6.55lb/in² (0.46kg/cm²).
Power to weight ratio: 13.8hp/ton.
Engine: GAZ-202 six-cylinder water-cooled petrol engine developing 70hp at 2,800rpm.
Performance: Road speed 28mph (45km/h); range 382 miles (615km); vertical obstacle 1ft 9in (0.54m); trench 6ft 1in (1.85m); gradient 60 per cent.
History: In service with the Russian Army from 1941 to 1945.

In 1941 the T-60 light tank appeared as a replacement for the T-40 light amphibious tank. In this case, however, because of the need for much heavier armour, the tank was a purely land-based vehicle. Experience gained during the first months of the Russo-German War had shown that high mobility and an amphibious capability were not all that were needed in battle. Designers in Soviet tank factories therefore took steps to increase the armour and firepower on the light tank. As the result they developed the T-60 light tank with 20mm (0.79in) armour on the front. The greatest stumbling block, however, was the provision of more powerful armament. Soviet engineers attempted to mount a 37mm gun but, even with a reduced charge round, the turret ring was incapable of absorbing the recoil of this weapon. The Soviet armament designer B. Shpital'n was therefore given the task of developing a special high-powered weapon for the tank. He developed the rapid-firing 20mm ShVAK-20 gun. Despite the reduced calibre, the armour-piercing incendiary round of this gun possessed the same armour-penetration qualities as the original 37mm gun. It fired a heavy soft-core round incorporating a sub-calibre slug. In comparison with previous light-tank models, the hull front and turret had improved protection against heavy-calibre machine-gun rounds, and although cast

armour had been adopted for the medium and heavy tank classes and for the turret of the T-50 light tank, both hull and turret of the T-60 were welded throughout.

The T-60 entered production during November 1941 and over 6,000 were produced before the type was supplanted by the successor T-70 light tank. The vehicle was issued to reconnaissance units and also to infantry units for direct infantry support. The turret was offset to the left, with the engine mounted alongside it on the right and the driver was placed centrally in the front. An improved model of the T-60 was produced in late 1941/early 1942, and this was designated T-60A. It had increased armour, but the main external difference lay in the wheels. The T-60 had spoked road-wheels and rollers whilst those on the T-60A were pressed solid. When eventually replaced by the more powerful T-70 light tank, the T-60 chassis were employed as mountings for M-8 and M-13 (Katyusha) rocket-launchers, and also as artillery tractors for 57mm anti-tank guns.

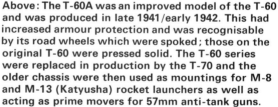

Above: The T-60A was an improved model of the T-60 and was produced in late 1941/early 1942. This had increased armour protection and was recognisable by its road wheels which were spoked; those on the original T-60 were pressed solid. The T-60 series were replaced in production by the T-70 and the older chassis were then used as mountings for M-8 and M-13 (Katyusha) rocket launchers as well as acting as prime movers for 57mm anti-tank guns.

Left: The T-60 entered production in November 1941 as the replacement for the T-40 light amphibious tank and over 6,000 were eventually built. The T-60 was not amphibious, as experience during the first few months of the Russo-German War had shown that high mobility and an amphibious capability were not all that were needed in battle. The T-60 was armed with a 20mm ShVAK-20 gun which fired an armour piercing round with the same penetration qualities as a 37mm gun — which was quite an achievement.

T-34 Medium Tank

A-20, T-32, T-34, T-34/76 and T-34/85.
Country of origin: Soviet Union.
Crew: 5.
Armament: One 85mm M1944 Z1S S53 L/51 gun; two 7.62mm DT machine-guns.
Armour: 18mm to 60mm (0.71in to 2.36in).
Dimensions: Length (including gun) 24ft 7in (7.5m); width 9ft 7in (2.92m); height 7ft 10in (2.39m).
Weight: 70,547lbs (32,000kg).
Ground Pressure: 11.2lb/in^2 (0.8kg/cm^2).
Power to weight ratio: 15.9hp/ton.
Engine: One V-2-34 12-cylinder water-cooled diesel developing 500hp at 1,800rpm.
Performance: Road speed 31mph (50km/h); range 186 miles (300km); vertical obstacle 2ft 7in (0.79m); trench 8ft 2in (2.49m); gradient 60 per cent.
History: In service with the Russian Army from 1940. Still used by many countries today.

During 1936 the young engineer M. I. Koshkin was transferred to the Komintern Factory in Kharkov as chief designer. The design bureau of the factory had been concerned with the continued modernisation of the *BT* wheel/track tank. At the beginning of 1937 this factory was assigned the task of designing a new medium tank, also a wheel/track design, designated A-20. The design of this tank was completed in November of that year. The 17.7 ton (18,000kg) A-20, armed with a 45mm gun, was the first of the so-called 'Shellproof Tanks', having greatly inclined armour, a characteristic feature of the later T-34 tank. The chassis was similar to that used on the *BT* tank but with certain automotive changes. A further version, mounting a 76.2mm gun, was developed and designated A-30.

In the meantime, Koshkin had come to the conclusion that to produce the new medium tank as a wheel/track vehicle was erroneous. The Red Army had seldom if ever used the *BT* tank in the wheeled mode, and to incorporate this facility required complication of design and severe weight penalties. He therefore proposed the development of a purely tracked variant, designated

A-32 (later T-32). The Main Military Council of the USSR accepted this proposal and authorised the construction of a prototype. They had not, however, yet dismissed the wheel/track project and awaited comparison trials at a later date. Prototypes of the A-20 and T-32 tanks were completed at Kharkov at the beginning of 1939, and during that year were exhibited to the Armoured Directorate. The Directorate recommended an increase in armour on the T-32 and the adoption of more powerful armament. The group under Koshkin achieved this, the final variant being called T-34. ▶

Right and below: A T-34/76B which appeared in 1941. It was basically a commander's T-34/76A with a rolled plate turret armed with a more powerful Model 1940 76.2mm L/41.5 gun for which a total of 77 rounds of ammunition were carried. A 7.62mm DT machine gun was mounted co-axial with the main armament and a second 7.62mm mounted in hull to right of the driver. The commander's tank was often the only one in a company with a radio.

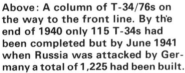

Above: A column of T-34/76s on the way to the front line. By the end of 1940 only 115 T-34s had been completed but by June 1941 when Russia was attacked by Germany a total of 1,225 had been built.

Right: The T-34/85 had a larger turret and was armed with the potent 85mm D-5T gun. It entered production in 1944.

Due to the serious international situation, on 19 December 1939, before the completion of a prototype, the Main Military Council accepted the T-34 project for equipping the armoured units of the Red Army. Towards the end of January 1940, the first production models of the T-34, designated T-34 06 1940, were released from the Komintern Factory. At the beginning of February two of these underwent a trial march, under the personal supervision of Koshkin. During June 1940, the manufacturing drawings were completed and the tank entered mass production. Since Koshkin had been taken ill, his assistant A. A. Morozov had taken over the final design.

The T-34 (called *Prinadlezhit-Chetverki* or 'Thirty-Four' by the troops) was noted for its excellently shaped armour, which considerably increased its resistance to shell penetration. The armament, a 76.2mm long-barrelled high-velocity gun, was also an innovation for tanks of this class. The use of the new 500hp V-2 diesel engine (already in service on the *BT-7M* tank) reduced the fire risk and greatly increased the operational range of the tank. The modified Christie suspension permitted high speeds, even on rough terrain, and the wide tracks reduced the ground pressure to a minimum. The overall design of the tank facilitated rapid mass production and lent itself to simple maintenance and repair in the field.

By the end of 1940 115 T-34s had been produced. Some were dispatched to Finland for combat tests but arrived too late to participate in operations. By June 1941, when the Germans attacked, a total of 1,225 had been produced. By the Battle of Moscow, 1,853 had been delivered to units, but of

course many of these had since been destroyed. The T-34 made its combat debut on 22 June 1941, in the vicinity of Grodno (Belorussia). It was a complete surprise to the German Army, who learned to treat this tank with the greatest respect. The question was raised of manufacturing a copy of it in Germany, but this proved impracticable. As the result, the Germans developed their famous Panther tank, whose general design was greatly influenced by that of the T-34. With the evacuation of the Soviet tank industry to the east, subsequent production of the T-34 was carried out at the *Uralmashzavod* (Ural Machine-Building Plant) in the Urals, as well as a number of subsidiary plants generally safe from German bombing.

The T-34 tank was originally armed with the 76.2mm Model 1939 L-11 gun mounted in a welded turret of rolled plate. In order to accelerate production, a new cast turret was soon introduced. During mid-1941 a new Model 40 F-34 gun was adopted. This had a longer barrel and higher muzzle velocity. A multiplicity of minor and major changes were made to the T-34 during production, but the most significant took place in autumn 1943, when the 85mm 215 S-53 or D-5T gun, with 55 rounds, was adopted. Some 2,394 rounds of 7.62mm ammunition were also carried. This new tank was called T-34/85 and was approved for mass production on 15 December 1943. By the end of the year 283 had been built, and in the following year a further 11,000 were produced. The T-34/85 remained in production until the mid-1950s, when the T-54 was adopted. It served with other armies as late as the mid-1960s. In the 1970s China used the T-34 chassis for an SPAA weapon.

T-70 Light Tank

T-70 and T-70A.
Country of origin: Soviet Union.
Crew: 2.
Armament: One 45mm L/46 gun; one 7.62mm DT machine-gun.
Armour: 0.39in (10mm) minimum; 2.36in (60mm) maximum.
Dimensions: Length 15ft 3in (5m); width 7ft 8in (2.52m); height 6ft 9in (2.22m).
Weight: 21,958lbs (9,960kg).
Ground Pressure: 9.53lb/in² (0.67kg/cm²).
Power to weight ratio: 14.29hp/ton.
Engine: Two Z1S-202 six-cylinder water-cooled petrol engines each developing 70hp at 2,800rpm.
Performance: Road speed 32mph (51km/h); range 279 miles (446km); vertical obstacle 2ft 2in (0.71m); trench 9ft 6in (3.12m); gradient 70 per cent.
History: In service with the Red Army from 1942 to 1948.

During late January 1942 the T-70 light tank began to replace the T-60 model in Russian service. Despite the fact that it had been shown that the light tank was not an effective vehicle, it was cheaper and easier to mass produce and this meant that units could receive tanks where they would otherwise have none. With the tremendous losses suffered by the Soviet tank parks during the first six months of the war (put at over 18,000 vehicles) and the fact that most of the Soviet tank industry had to be transferred to the central regions of the USSR, thereby delaying production, any tank production was imperative. As the war progressed, however, the production of medium and heavy tanks soon reached the desired level and the final light tank model to enter service remained the T-70. The T-70 light tank was mass produced at the Gorki Automobile Works. It replaced the T-60 in light tank units.

The T-70 had the same chassis as the T-60 (with the drive taken to the front, instead of the rear), slightly reinforced to take the extra weight, but mounted a 45mm gun (with 70 rounds) and co-axial 7.62mm DT machine-gun (with 945 rounds) in a new welded turret. The hull armour was also modified to give a cleaner outline and better protection, and the driver was provided with an armoured visor. The engine power was doubled by providing two engines of the type used in the T-60.

During mid-1943 the T-70A was produced. This was an improved version with increased armour and slightly more powerful engines. The turret, which was more heavily armoured, had a squared-off rear, as distinct from the rounded type of the T-70. Production of the T-70 and T-70A light tanks was discontinued in the autumn of 1943 as the result of increased medium tank output. Altogether, 8,226 of the T-70 light tank were turned out. In 1944 the surviving chassis were modified (an extra bogie wheel on each side) and converted to self-propelled gun mountings.

Right: The T-70 was introduced as the successor to the T-60 light tank and had the same chassis but with drive sprocket at the front instead of the rear. It was armed with a 45mm gun in place of a 20mm cannon. To cope with the increased weight the T-70 was powered by two ZIS-202 petrol engines developing 70hp each. By the time it was introduced the Soviets had realised that the value of the light tank was limited compared to that of the medium tank such as the T-34 but as there were insufficient of these to equip all tank units production of the T-70 was allowed to continue for a few years. Many of the surviving T-70s were subsequently converted into SU-76 SPGs.

Above: The T-70A was introduced in 1942 and differed from the T-70 in having a more heavily armoured turret with squared off rear, as distinct from the rounded type of the original model, and more powerful engines. Production of the T-70 was completed in 1944 after some 8,226 had been built.

IS-2 Heavy Tank

IS-1, IS-2 and IS-3.
Country of origin: Soviet Union.
Crew: 4.
Armament: One 122mm M1943 (D-25) L/43 tank gun; one 12.7mm M1938 DShK machine-gun; one 7.62mm DT or DTM machine-gun.
Armour: 132mm (5.2in) maximum; 19mm (0.75in) minimum.
Dimensions: Length (including gun) 32ft 9in (10.74m); width 10ft 6in (3.44m); height 8ft 11in (2.93m).
Weight: 101,963lbs (46,250kg).
Ground Pressure: 11.25lb/in^2 (0.79kg/cm^2).
Power to weight ratio: 11.3hp/ton.
Engine: One Model V-2 IS 12-cylinder water-cooled diesel developing 520hp at 2,000rpm.
Performance: Road speed 23mph (37km/h); range 94 miles (150km); vertical obstacle 3ft 3in (1m); trench 8ft 2in (2.86m); gradient 70 per cent.
History: In service with the Russian Army from 1943 to late 1970s.

In August 1942 the Soviet high command was well aware of the fact that Germany was developing new heavy tanks with more powerful armament and thicker armour. Work on a new heavy tank was therefore begun. Based on the experience gained so far in the design of experimental KV models (KV-3 and KV-13), in 1943 the design bureau investigated a new project designated IS (Iosef Stalin). Early in autumn 1943 the first three prototypes of the IS-1 (also called IS-85 because of its 85mm gun) were completed. After demonstration before the special commission from the Main Defence Commissariat and the completion of general factory trials, the IS design was approved. Directions were given to begin mass-production in October 1943.

The new tank, weighing little more than the KV (and for that matter, the German Panther medium tank) had thicker, better shaped armour which provided excellent protection. In addition, the weight was kept low by the use of more compact component design. The tank had a new cast turret

mounting an 85mm gun specially designed by General F. Petrov (the same turret as fitted to the KV-85 as an expedient). Soon after the start of production of the IS-1 tank, the need arose for a more powerfully armed vehicle. At that time the 85mm gun was being used in the T-34 medium (T-34/85) and it was considered inappropriate that a heavy tank should have the same armament. A few prototypes were therefore fitted with a new 100mm gun (IS-100), but were not accepted for production. This was because another group, under General Petrov, had within two weeks conceived a scheme for mounting a 122mm gun (with 28 rounds). Towards the end of October 1943 factory and proving ground tests were concluded for the IS tank fitted with this weapon. On 31 October the tank was accepted as standard and designated IS-2. By the end of the year the Kirov Factory had produced 102 IS-2 tanks.

The IS tank was used for the first time during February 1944 at Korsun Shevkenskovsky. During this battle General Kotin personally observed the performance of the IS-2 tank and gained vital information as to its performance and short-comings. After producing several other experimental vehicles of this type, work on a further improvement to the armour layout led, towards the end of 1944, to the new IS-3 model. The design of this tank, carried out by a group under N. Dukhov, was conceived around the armour philosophy of the T-34. Armour plate of even greater thickness and better ballistic shape was heavily inclined to give maximum protection. In contrast to its predecessors, the IS-3 hull was made of rolled plate and the turret was carapace-shaped. Despite all these improvements, the overall weight of the new tank still did not exceed that of the contemporary German medium tank. The final model of this heavy tank, T-10, was the tenth model to be produced. The prefix 'IS' was discontinued as a result of the general de-Stalinisation policy adopted in the Soviet Union during the mid-1950s.

Below: IS-2 heavy tank on the Leningrad front. The IS-2 was accepted for service on 31 October 1943 and by the end of that year the Kirov factory had built 102. By the end of 1944 a total of 2,250 had been completed. Further development resulted in the IS-3 which entered service in January 1945.

UNITED STATES

The United States Tank Corps was established in France in early 1918 and was equipped with British and French tanks. Thus, as the USA had no tank design experience, the American army followed very much the same approach to armoured warfare in the early 1920s as did the French and the British: light tanks for reconnaissance and heavy, slow-moving tanks for immediate infantry support in the assault.

In fact, the Tank Corps was disbanded in 1920, and all tanks were assigned to the infantry where they were to remain until the formation of the Armored Force in 1940. Between 1920 and 1935 fewer than 40 tanks were built in the United States. The urgent need for rearmament was only clearly seen in 1940 and, without further revision, some unsuitable designs were put into production. Even then the full impact of the German use of armour was not appreciated, until General Chaffee began to point it out in clear and positive terms. It was he who put the US Armored Force on the right footing to go to war, and the lesson he rammed home was that of the combined arms team. He was justified in Tunisia and later in Sicily, where the value of firepower and mobility were also amply demonstrated.

The first US tank to be built in quantity was the M2A2 light tank, of which 170 were produced by 1937. Further development resulted in the M2A4 (329 ordered in October 1939), but it was not until medium tank development had

gathered pace that really significant numbers were coming off the production lines. By May 1940 just 18 M2 medium tanks had been completed; then it was realised that a medium tank with a 75mm gun would be needed, so an M2 prototype chassis was fitted with a sponson-mounted 75mm gun as there was no time in which to design a turret.

It soon became apparent that one advantage the USA had over most Allies (and enemies) was that it could gear up its manufacturing capabilities to suit the need of the moment: between 1940 and 1942 there were 6,000 75mm-gunned M2 mediums (standardised as the M3 Grant) built, and no sooner had this entered production than work had started on a tank armed with a 75mm turret-mounted gun. This was standardised as the Sherman, and no fewer than 48,000 were produced between 1942 and 1945. By the end of the war, the US built 88,000 tanks compared to 24,000 built by Britain and Germany, owing much of course to the safety of its industry from enemy air attack.

The great lesson that American armour taught the world during the war, however, was that successful tanks are those that are easy to maintain and reliable in action. The M4 Sherman may have lacked many battle qualities, but it was very straightforward and relatively simple for its crew to manage, and what it lacked in effectiveness was more than made up in sheer numbers.

M3 Light Tank

M3, M3A1, M3A2 and M3A3.
Country of origin: United States.
Crew: 4.
Armament: One 37mm M5 or M6 gun; one .3in M1919A4 machine-gun co-axial with main armament; two .3in machine-guns in hull sponsons; one .3in machine-gun on turret roof.
Armour: 44.5mm (1.75in) maximum; 10mm (0.375in) minimum.
Dimensions: Length 14ft 10½in (4.53m); width 7ft 4in (2.23m); height 8ft 3in (2.51m).
Weight: Combat 27,400lbs (12,428kg).
Ground pressure: 10.5lb/in² (0.74kg/cm²).
Power to weight ratio: 20.4hp/ton.
Engine: Continental W-670 seven-cylinder air-cooled radial petrol engine developing 250hp at 2,400rpm.
Performance: Road speed 36mph (58km/h); cross-country speed 20mph (32km/h); road range 70 miles (112km); vertical obstacle 2ft (0.6m); trench 6ft (1.8m); fording depth 3ft (0.9m); gradient 60 per cent.
History: Entered service with US Army in 1941. Also widely used by British and other Allied armies during World War II. *continued* ▶

Below: Stuart Mark I light tank of the 8th (King's Royal Irish) Hussars, at the Battle of Sidi Rezegh in November 1941. The M3 was the first American-built tank to be used in action by the British Army during the war. The 8th Army in North Africa received its first shipment of 84 Lend-Lease M3s in July 1941 and by November the same year 163 were ready for Operation Crusader. The M3 was officially called the General Stuart in British Army service but was commonly known as the Stuart or Honey. Some later had their turrets removed for use in command role.

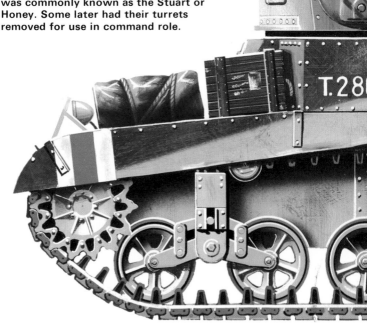

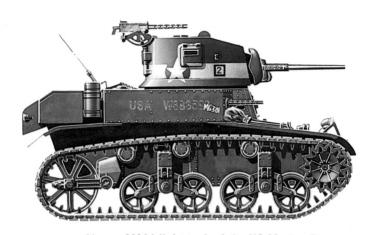

Above: M3A1 light tank of the US Marine Corps on Guadalcanal Island in the Solomons, September 1942. Clearly shown in this drawing is the .3in M1919A4 machine gun on the turret roof and one of the two sponson-mounted M1919A4 machine guns. The latter were often removed to allow for more internal stowage space, always at a premium in any AFV. Production of the M3 was finally completed in October 1943 after 13,859 tanks had been built.

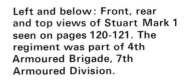

Left and below: Front, rear and top views of Stuart Mark 1 seen on pages 120-121. The regiment was part of 4th Armoured Brigade, 7th Armoured Division.

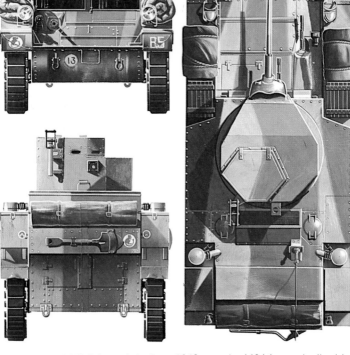

The standard US light tank in June 1940 was the M2A4, standardised in 1939 and the culmination of a development which began with the M2A1 in 1935. The M2A4 weighed some 12 tons (12,193kg), had a 37mm turret-mounted gun and was constructed from riveted armour plate. Increasing the thickness of the armour of the M2A4 called for the use of a trailing idler in the suspension system. This, with improved protection from aircraft attack, led to the standardisation of the type as the M3 light tank in July 1940. The Continental seven-cylinder radial engine of 250hp had been inherited from the M2A4, but in 1941 shortages of this engine meant that the Guiberson T-1020 diesel engine was authorised for 500 M3 light tanks. Additional fuel capacity in the form of two external fuel tanks, which could be jettisoned, was provided as a result of battle experience in British hands in North Africa.

The M3 was produced in quantity by the American Car and Foundry Company, 5,811 having been built by August 1942. The M3A1 light tank incorporated an improved turret of welded homogeneous plate (as opposed to the earlier brittle, face-hardened armour) with power traverse, a gyro-stabiliser to permit more accurate firing of the 37mm gun on the move, and a turret basket. The M3A1 was standardised in August 1941 and used the hull of the M3, which was still constructed from riveted plate. A pilot with both hull and turret formed of welded armour, the M3A1E1, led eventually to the M5 light tank. The next model, the M3A2, was also to be of welded construction but similar to the M3A1 in all other respects. The M3A2 was not built, but American Car and Foundry produced 4,621 of the M3A1, of which 211 were diesel-engined. The M3A3 was a much more comprehensive redesign and included changes in the turret, hull and sponsons, and it was considered worthwhile to continue producing the M3A3 even after the production line for its successor, the M5, was established. Some 3,427 M3A3s were built. There were several experimental models of the M3 series, mostly involving different automotive installations.

In British service the M3 provided a much-needed addition to the tank strength in the Western Desert in 1941 and 1942. It subsequently appeared in all theatres of World War II, but is chiefly remembered for its service in the desert, with the empire forces in Burma, in the capture of Antwerp, and with the American forces in the Pacific. It was under-gunned and poorly armoured but mobile and reliable, and was affectionately known as the 'Honey' by British cavalry regiments. Indeed, many units preferred it to the Daimler armoured car in the reconnaissance role. The M3 was the most widely used light tank of World War II and was built in larger numbers than its two successors, the M5 and M24. A total of 13,859 had been produced by October 1943, even though the type had been declared obsolete in July of that year. Although it was fast and had good ground-crossing ability for the 'cavalry' scouting role for which it was intended, the M3 had little scope for development or adaptation. The hull was too narrow, effectively limiting the size of the main armament to below the required 75mm, and it was too high and angular, offering a high silhouette and many shot traps. It did lead directly to the M5 light tank, however, and its history continued under that heading.

Below: The M3 light tank was developed from the earlier M2 shown here with its higher rear idler wheel. The M2 was designed and built at Rock Island Arsenal with the first model, the M2A1, being standardised in late 1935. In addition to the prototype, just 19 production M2A1s were built.

M3 Grant/Lee Medium Tank

M3, M3A1, M3A2, M3A3, M3A4, M3A5, and variants.
Country of origin: United States.
Crew: 6.
Armament: One 75mm M2 or M3 gun in hull sponson; one 37mm M5 or M6 gun in turret; one .3in M1919A4 machine-gun co-axial with turret gun; one .3in machine-gun in cupola on turret; two .3in machine-guns in bow.
Armour: 12mm to 37mm.
Dimensions: Length 18ft 6in (5.64m); width 8ft 11in (2.72m); height 10ft 3in (3.12m).
Weight: Combat 60,000lbs (27,216kg).
Ground Pressure: 13.4lb/in² (0.94kg/cm²).
Power to weight ratio: 12.7hp/ton.
Engine: Wright Continental R-975-EC2 nine-cylinder air-cooled radial petrol engine developing 340hp at 2,400rpm.
Performance: Road speed 26mph (42km/h); cross-country speed 16mph (26km/h); road range 120 miles (193km); vertical obstacle 2ft (0.6m); trench 6ft 3in (1.9m); gradient 60 per cent.
History: Entered service with US Army and British Army in 1941. Also used by Canadian and Russian armies.

Battlefield experience reported from Europe in 1939 showed that the 37mm gun of the American M2 medium tank was not powerful enough for modern warfare, and accordingly the 75mm pack howitzer was experimentally mounted in the right-hand sponson of the Medium Tank T5 Phase III, a vehicle closely related to the M2. Such a vehicle would previously have been classed as a howitzer motor carriage. Meanwhile, in the United States rearmament programme William S. Knudsen, president of the General Motors Corporation, had been co-opted to the National Defense Advisory Committee to co-ordinate the capabilities of industry to the needs of defence.

The existing contract for 329 M2A4 light tanks was clearly insufficient and industry did not seem able to cope with the order for 1,500 M2 medium tanks which was then envisaged. In 1940 it was suggested that the M2 be ▶

Left: While the 75mm gun of the Grant was a great improvement over that installed in other tanks used by the British Army it was sponson-mounted on the right side and therefore only had a total traverse of 30°. The tank had tractor-type ('scissors') suspension, in common with most US tanks until late in the war. A total of 6,258 M3s were built for the Allied Armies.

Above: M3 Grant medium tank negotiating rough terrain. In October 1940 the British Tank Commission placed orders with Baldwin and Pullman in the United States for 200 M3 Grant tanks. These were all shipped to the 8th Army in North Africa with first tanks arriving in early 1942. During the battle of Gazala in May 1942, 167 Grants formed the main equipment of the 4th Armoured Brigade and at last gave the British Army a tank that could outrange those used by the German Africa Korps, but the tank had several weak features. The M3 was also used by Canada and the Soviet Union.

Left: Grant tank fitted with a dummy lorry body as a disguise in North Africa. In addition to being used as a tank, many M3s were modified for special roles including tank recovery vehicle, full-track prime mover for 155mm gun, mine exploder (trials), 3 inch gun motor carriage (trials), 40mm gun motor carriage (trials), heavy tractor (trials) and also as the basis for the 105mm M7 Priest.

Right: Top view of M3 Grant medium tank clearly showing the multiplicity of weapons with which the vehicle was armed, arranged in three tiers. The tank commander could operate the .30 Browning machine gun in the independently-rotating cast cupola, while the turret gunner could engage armour with the 37mm anti-tank gun or infantry with the co-axial Browning machine gun, and the 75mm M2 or M3 hull-mounted gun could fire either AP or HE ammunition. This M3 is of all-riveted construction but others (eg, the M3A1) had a cast hull. There were very many experimental non-tank variants of the M3.

improved by increasing its armour and adapting the 75mm M1897 gun (as the T7) to a sponson mounting in the hull. This new tank was designated the M3 medium tank by the Ordnance Committee on 11 July 1940, and on 28 August 1940 the contract for 1,000 M2A1 medium tanks, signed only 15 days previously, was changed in favour of the M3.

Up to this point, America's tank needs had been met largely by the heavy engineering industry. Knudsen, now a lieutenant-general, took the view that apart from the manufacturing and casting of armour, there was little difference between manufacturing a car and a tank. He therefore arranged with K. T. Keller, president of the Chrysler Corporation, for Chrysler to lease a 113-acre (45.73-hectare) site for a new tank factory. The site at Warren, Michigan, was to become the government-owned, Chrysler-operated arsenal responsible for the production of some 25,000 armoured vehicles during World War II. The M3 was ordered into production from the drawing board and Chrysler, the American Locomotive Company (Alco) and the Baldwin Locomotive Works all produced pilot models by April 1941. Production began in August 1941 and continued until December 1942, by which time 6,258 vehicles of the M3 series had been built. Of this total Chrysler built 3,352, Alco 685, Baldwin 1,220, Pressed Steel 501 and Pullman 500. These figures are quoted to illustrate what was basically the first application of motorcar mass-production techniques to tank production.

During production it became necessary to make various modifications to overcome shortages and to improve the tank. The M3A1 used a cast hull produced by Alco, this hull having no side doors for reasons of strength. A welded hull, stronger than the riveted hull of the M3, was used to save weight in the M3A2, of which Baldwin built 12. Baldwin also built 322 of the M3A3 which used two General Motors 6-71 diesel bus engines coupled together as an alternative to the Wright radial engine. Otherwise the M3A3 was identical to the M3A2. The M3, M3A1 and M3A2 could also be fitted with a Guiberson diesel engine, in which case the designation became, for example, M3A1 (Diesel). To overcome a critical shortage of the Wright engine in 1941, Chrysler combined five standard car engines to provide a tank powerpack. This 'Eggbeater' engine required modifications to the hull and suspension, resulting in the M3A4. The hull was riveted as in the M3, and 109 were built. The M3A5 resulted from the installation of the twin GM diesels of the M3A3 in the riveted hull of the M3, and Baldwin built 591.

In British service the M3 was known as the Grant (after General Ulysses S. Grant) and the Lee (after General Robert E. Lee). A British Tank Commission had arrived in June 1940 with the intention of ordering British-designed tanks from American firms. But as at that time the defeat of the British appeared imminent, the National Defense Advisory Committee refused to allow tanks to be produced to British designs. As a result of this refusal the M3 was chosen as being the next best choice. Those purchased by the British Tank Commission from Pullman and Pressed Steel had a British-designed turret and were known as Grant I. The name Lee was given to the standard M3 (Lee I), M3A1 (Lee II), M3A3 (Lee IV), M3A3 (Diesel) (Lee V), and M3A4 (Lee VI), while the M3A5 was known as the Grant II, these tanks being supplied under the terms of the 1941 Lend-Lease Act.

The Grant I had its first impact at the battle of Gazala on 27 May 1942, the first time the 8th Army had managed to achieve any degree of parity with the

75mm gun of the *PzKpfw* IV, although it was some time before problems associated with fuses for the HE shell could be resolved. By October 1942 a further 350 M3s had been supplied and these tanks made a significant contribution to the success at El Alamein in November of that year. Some M3s were shipped to the UK for training units, but the majority were used in North Africa and the Middle East.

By April 1943 the M4 was in full production, and the M3 was finally declared obsolete on 16 March 1944. Despite this the M3 lived on in the form of variants such as the M7 'Priest' and the M31 Tank Recovery Vehicle. The chassis was also used for many experimental variations, including: Mine Exploder T1, Tank Recovery Vehicle T2 (M31), 155mm Gun Motor Carriage T6 (M12), Shop Tractor T10 (Canal Defense Light, or searchlight tank), Cargo Carrier T14, Heavy Tractor T16, 3in Gun Motor Carriage T24, 105mm Howitzer Motor Carriage T25, 75mm Gun Motor Carriage T26, 105mm Howitzer Motor Carriage T32 (M7 'Priest'), 40mm Gun Motor Carriage T36, 3in Gun Motor Carriage T40 (M9), 25pounder Gun Motor Carriage T51, Flamethrower Vehicles (several were made, using the E3 and M5R2 flame guns). Vehicles of the M3 series supplied to the British Army were also modified for various purposes, for example as recovery vehicles, command vehicles, mineclearing vehicles, and as a canal defence light.

M4 Sherman Medium Tank

Country of origin: United States.
Crew: 5.
Armament: One 75mm M3 gun; one .3in M1919A4 machine-gun co-axial with main armament; one .3in M1919A4 machine-gun in ball mount in bow; one .5in M2 machine-gun on turret roof; one 2in M3 smoke mortar in turret roof.
Armour: 0.6in (15mm) minimum; 3.94in (100mm) maximum.
Dimensions: Length 20ft 7in (6.27m); width 8ft 11in (2.67m); height 11ft 1in (3.37m).
Weight: Combat 69,565lbs (31,554kg).
Ground Pressure: 14.3lb/in^2 (1kg/cm^2).
Power to weight ratio: 16.9hp/ton.
Engine: Ford GAA V-8 water-cooled inline petrol engine developing 500hp at 2,600rpm.
Performance: Road speed 26mph (42km/h); road range 100 miles (160km); vertical obstacle 2ft (0.61m); trench 7ft 6in (2.29m); fording depth 3ft (0.91m); gradient 60 per cent.
History: Entered service in 1942, and saw extensive service with US Army and most Allied armies during and after World War II. The most prolific medium tank of World War II, and widely adapted to other uses. Also used in action in Korea and Middle East and still in service with some armies. (Note: Data relate to a typical M4A3.)

On 29 August 1940, the day following the decision to produce the M3 medium tank in place of the M2A1, work began on a new medium tank which would mount the 75mm gun in a turret with a full 360° traverse. The new tank was designated the T6 medium tank, and its design was based on the use of components of the M3 as far as possible. Elimination of the sponson mount would reduce the hull space enclosed by armour, and thus reduce weight or ▶

Below: Side view of M4A3E8, known as to the Americans as the "Easy Eight" because of its HVSS suspension which gave a good ride across country. The vehicle is shown as it appeared on ceremonial parade with the United States Occupation Forces in Munich, South Germany, in June 1945.

Above: A posed photograph of a
US Army M4 Sherman with infantry "fighting" from the rear of
the tank. This was a wide practice
in the Soviet Army but in other
armies the infantry normally
followed behind the tank on foot.
The white band around the turret
of this Sherman indicates that
it is a command tank.

permit a greater thickness of armour. The T6 was standardised in September 1941 as the M4 medium tank, but in all its many models it was more widely and popularly known as the 'Sherman'.

As adopted, the Sherman weighed about 30 tons (30,482kg) and was armed with the 75mm M2 gun. The turret was a one-piece rounded casting, 3in (76.2mm) thick at the front, and power operated. A gyrostabiliser controlled the gun in elevation. The lower hull was welded, while the construction of the upper hull provided a certain degree of identification of the various models. The M4 had a welded upper hull, while the M4A1 had a cast, rounded upper hull. Both were approximately 2in (50.8mm) thick. Variations between the major models in the M4 series were mainly due to different engine installations, apart from the difference in hull construction in the case of the M4 and M4A1.

Production of the Sherman was authorised to replace the M3 as soon as possible. Facilities involved included the Chrysler-operated Detroit Arsenal, the Fisher Body Division of GMC, the Ford Motor Company, Pacific Car and Foundry, Federal Machine and Welder Company, Lima Locomotive Works and the Montreal Locomotive Works, and 49,230 Shermans of all variants were produced. Product improvement was a continuous process throughout, and indeed after production had ceased. The most significant improvements centred on armament, stowage of ammunition and suspension.

The gun conceived for the T6 medium tank prototype was the un-satisfactory 75mm T6 gun. The next model, the T7, was better and became the 75mm M2 gun in May 1941, but was still relatively short-barrelled and had a muzzle velocity of only 1,850fps (564m/s). Early models of the Sherman had the M2 gun, but even in September 1940 the Armoured Force had requested a higher muzzle velocity, and this request was met in the 75mm T8 gun, adopted in June 1941 as the M3. This gun fired armour-piercing shot at a muzzle velocity of 2,030tps (619m/s) and was also more suited to tank use. The longer barrel was better balanced for installation in a gyrostabiliser mount and rotation of the breech to allow the block to open horizontally permitted greater depression of the gun in a turret mount.

Although the 75mm gun was accepted as the standard weapon, the Ordnance Department felt that more penetrating power would be required.

The 3in gun of the M6 heavy tank was not ideal, but adapting the 75mm breech to the 3in barrel produced a most satisfactory weapon. At first known as the 3in T13 gun but later as the 76mm T1 gun, this weapon was mounted on the Sherman in a project which began in August 1942. The project, although promising, found no support and was dropped in November of the same year. Later the T23 medium tank turret, with the 76mm gun, was mounted on the Sherman. The improvement was so marked that the Armored Board admitted to a requirement for 76mm guns to supplant 75mm guns when the extra firepower was needed. This was a face-saving gesture to allow production to begin after the earlier refusal. The fact that by July 1944 over 2,000 76mm gun tanks had been produced illustrates just how much the extra firepower was needed — and this after vehicles armed with the 76mm gun had been declared obsolete in May 1943!

Another innovation in armament concerned the 105mm howitzer. In April 1941 the Aberdeen Proving Ground had suggested that the Sherman would conveniently mount the 105mm howitzer, but it was not until late 1942 that two M4A4s were modified for this purpose. Further tests were carried out on a similarly modified vehicle, the M4E5, and the howitzer in the M52 mount ▶

Right and below: Front and rear views of M4A3E8 with insignia: from left to right, denoting 7th Army, 191st Tank Batt., A Company, Tank No. 12. Top view shows gun travelling lock on glacis plate. Lower view shows .5in M2 MG stowed to turret rear.

Left: The M4A3E8 Sherman mounting a 105mm howitzer with which it gave close support to the medium tank formations of the US Army, replacing the older M8 75mm SP howitzer. This Sherman has a welded hull, cast turret with commander's cupola and HVSS suspension. Over 4,600 105mm armed M4 Shermans were built from 1943. The 105mm M4 howitzer had an elevation of +35° and a depression of −10°, 66 rounds of 105mm ammunition being carried.

Above: Rear view of Red Army Shermans before Kharkov in 1943. Note the applique armour on the hull side below turret and the fuel drums at the hull rear to increase operating range.

was adopted as a standard item. These vehicles were used in headquarter companies to provide fire support and some 4,680 were built on the M4 and M4A3 hulls.

Early models of the Sherman had a somewhat unfortunate reputation for 'brewing-up' when hit by anti-tank fire. To overcome this fault attempts were made to protect the ammunition stowed in the tank. Stowage racks were provided in the lower hull and those for 75mm and 76mm ammunition were surrounded by water jackets, while the semi-fixed howitzer ammunition was protected by armour plate. The suffix 'wet' was added to nomenclature in May 1945 to distinguish those tanks with water jacket stowage.

To improve the ride and stability, and at the same time reduce the specific ground pressure of the Sherman, experiments were made with different suspensions and tracks. The original and highly characteristic vertical volute spring suspension of the Sherman series originated with the M2 medium tank, as did the 16in (0.41m) track, but both were more suited to a 20 ton (20,321kg) vehicle than the 30-plus tons of the M4. Eventually a new horizontal volute spring suspension and 23in (0.58m) track were perfected and incorporated in production. The suffix 'HVSS' was often added to designations to indicate the newer suspension.

The type lent itself to the production of many variants and most authorities list over 50 significant American experimental models. At least one of these is apparently still classified after 30 years. Tanks and other vehicles of the M4 series were supplied to many countries during and after World War II, and more Shermans were manufactured than any other single tank. Critics pointed out its deficiencies compared with the Panther, for example, but it made up for these shortcomings in reliability, endurance and sheer weight of numbers. Thirty-six years after its introduction the Sherman lives on in many armies and has appeared in almost every armoured conflict since 1945.

Above: the Sherman DD (Duplex Drive) was fitted with a flotation screen and propelled in the water by two propellers at the rear of the hull, these being driven by a PTO from the engine.

Below: The Sherman Firefly VC was a M4A4 re-armed in Britain with the 17-pounder gun, bussle fitted to turret and hull MG and gunner left out for increased ammunition stowage.

M24 Chaffee Light Tank

T17, M8, M8A1, T24, M24, M37, M19, M41, T77, T9, T13, T22, T23, T33, T42, T9, T6E1 and T31.

Country of origin: United States.

Crew 5, sometimes reduced to 4.

Armament: One 75mm M6 gun; one .3in M1919A4 machine-gun co-axial with main armament; one .3in M1919A4 machine-gun; one .5in M2 machine-gun; one 2in M3 smoke mortar.

Armour: 0.375in (10mm) minimum; 1.5in (38mm) maximum.

Dimensions: Length 18ft (5.49m); width 9ft 8in (2.95m); height 8ft 2in (2.77m).

Weight: Combat 40,500lbs (18,370kg).

Ground Pressure: 11.3lb/in² (0.79kg/cm²).

Power to weight ratio: 12.2hp/ton.

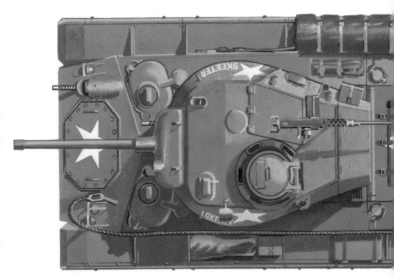

Engines: Two Cadillac 44T24 V-8 water-cooled petrol engines each developing 110hp at 3,400rpm.

Performance: Road speed 34mph (54km/h); road range 100 miles (160km); vertical obstacle 3ft (0.91m); trench 8ft (2.44m); fording depth 3ft 4in (1.02m) unprepared and 6ft 6in (1.98m) prepared; gradient 60 per cent.

History: Entered US Army service in 1944. Supplied to many other countries including (in small numbers) UK, and still in wide use in 1981. Basis of original 'Lightweight Combat Team'.

continued ▶

Below: Four views of the M24 Chaffee light tank used by the US Army in Europe from late 1944. Development of a new light tank to replace the M3 and M5 commenced in March 1943 and the M24 was in fact standardised in mid-1944 after it had already been in production for several months. By 1945 4,070 had been built. The French used the Chaffee in Vietnam in the 1950s.

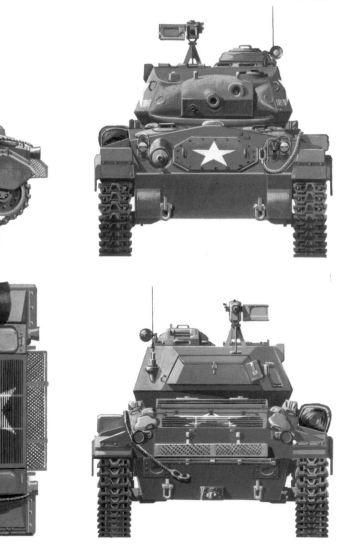

Compared with the M5 light tank which it replaced, the M24 was a quantum advance. In two of the three attributes of armour – firepower and protection – the M24 surpassed all other light tanks of World War II, while its mobility was comparable with the exceptionally agile M5. Its 75mm gun was almost the equal of that of the Sherman and more powerful than the armament of most medium tanks in 1939. The vastly improved hull and turret shape increased protection by the elimination of shot traps, reduction of the silhouette and better sloping of the armour. Today, it is normal to consider ease of maintenance as another attribute of the tank and the M24 was designed with accessibility of major assemblies in mind.

Military characteristics defined for the new light tank were that the power train of the M5A1 should be retained; the suspension should be improved; the gross weight should not exceed 16 long tons (16.257kg); and that the armour should reach a maximum of 1in (25.4mm) thickness and be acutely angled to the horizontal. The M5A1 light tank was limited in the space available within the turret, a fact which precluded the installation of the 75mm gun. A T21 light tank was considered, but at 21.5 tons (21,845kg) this would have been too heavy. The T7 light tank was examined exhaustively by the Armored Force. It had been designed around the 57mm gun at the request of the British Army and when the Armored Force asked for a 75mm gun, the resultant weight increase moved the T7 into the medium tank category. In fact standardisation as the M7 medium tank, with the 75mm gun, was approved but later cancelled to avoid the logistic disadvantages of having two standard medium tank types.

The Cadillac Motor Division of the General Motors Corporation delivered pilot models of a vehicle to meet the stated requirements in October 1943. The T24, as it was designated, was found satisfactory and 1,000 were ordered before service tests had begun. In addition, pilots of the T24E1 with the power train of the M18 tank destroyer were also ordered, but this development was later cancelled. The T24 mounted the T13E1 75mm gun in a Concentric Recoil Mechanism T33 with a .3in machine-gun in the Combination Gun Mount T90. The gun was a lightweight weapon developed from the M5 aircraft gun, and although the standardised nomenclature M6 was assigned, this merely indicated tank use as opposed to airborne use. The twin Cadillac engines of the T24 were mounted on rails for ease of maintenance – a feature of the T7 light tank – and were identical with those

Above: M24 Chaffee with wider tracks for use in muddy terrain at firing practice. The M24 was replaced in the US Army in the 1950s by the M41 Walker Bulldog.

Left: Although the M24 Chaffee light tank entered service as long ago as 1944, it is still, in 1981, used by many countries around the world, especially in the Far East and South America.

of the M5A1. Indeed, it was because the T24 shared the same power plant as the M5A1 that Cadillac was chosen to produce the T24 in quantity, although later American Car & Foundry and Massey-Harris were to be included in production.

The torsion-bar suspension of the M18 tank destroyer was used in the T24. Although the invention of this suspension is often ascribed to German tank designers, the American patent on torsion bar suspension was granted in December 1935 to G. M. Barnes and W. E. Preston. Five pairs of stamped disc wheels, 25in (63.5cm) in diameter and rubber-tired, were mounted on each side and a sprocket at the front drove the 16in (40.6cm) tracks. The hull of the T24 was of all welded construction, reaching a maximum thickness on frontal surfaces of 2.5in (63.5mm) although in less critical places the armour was thinner to conform to the concept of the light tank. A large cover in the glacis plate could be removed for access to the controlled differential steering, and dual controls were provided for the driver and assistant driver. In July 1944 the T24 was standardised as the M24 Light Tank, popularly known as the 'Chaffee', and by June 1945 a total of 4,070 had been produced.

In keeping with the idea of a Lightweight Combat Team, other vehicles using the M24 chassis were designed for specialist applications. A variety of gun and mortar carriages was developed, of which the T77 Multiple Gun Motor Carriage is one of the more interesting. A new turret mounting six .5in machine-guns was mounted on a basically standard M24 chassis and in a way this vehicle foreshadowed the modern six-barrelled Vulcan Air Defense System. Two armored utility vehicles, the T9 and T13, were designed and three cargo carriers also developed. The T22E1 and T23E1 were adaptations of the T22 and T23 which were based on the M5 light tank. The T33 Cargo Carrier was a later development which, with the substitution of the medium tank engine and torque converter transmission of the Hellcat, became the T42 Cargo Tractor. The T43 Cargo Tractor was a lighter version of the T42. A bulldozer kit, the T9, was developed and adopted as the M4 but was not widely used. Various aids to flotation were tried, as in the case of the Hellcat, but none was adopted for widespread use. Each of the Combat Team families was provided with a recovery vehicle, and the T6E1 Tank Recovery Vehicle was the model compatible with the M24 series. Although pilots were built, development was not pursued.

M26 Pershing Heavy Tank

T25, T26, T26E1, T26E2, T26E3, M26, M45, M46 and many variants.
Country of origin: United States.
Crew: 5.
Armament: One 90mm M3 gun; one .3in M1919A4 machine-gun co-axial with main armament; one .3in M1919A4 machine-gun in hull front; one .5in M2 machine-gun on turret roof.
Armour: 0.51in (13mm) minimum; 4in (102mm) maximum.
Dimensions: Length 28ft 5in (8.65m); width 11ft 6in (3.51m); height 9ft 1in (2.78m).
Weight: Combat 92,355lbs (41,891kg).
Ground Pressure: 13.1lb/in² (0.92kg/cm²).
Power to weight ratio: 10.9hp/ton.
Engine: Ford GAF V-8 water-cooled petrol engine developing 500hp at 2,600rpm.
Performance: Road speed 30mph (48km/h); road range 100 miles (160km); vertical obstacle 3ft 10in (1.17m); trench 8ft (2.44m); fording depth 4ft (1.22m); gradient 60 per cent.
History: Although doubts existed as to the need for such a tank, the Pershing entered US service in 1945. Saw service in Korea and in the 1950s with many foreign armies. Development of the M60 main battle tank can be traced to the M26.

When the M26 heavy tank was introduced into service with the US Army in 1945, it marked the end of a line of development which began in 1938 with the M2 medium tank. By the same token it marked the birth of a line culminating in the M60 series, the main battle tank of the 1960s.

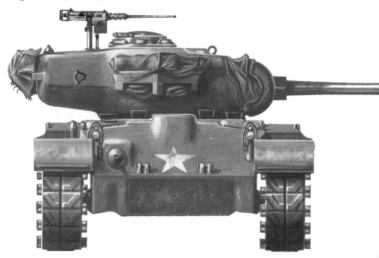

Above and right: Front and side views of M26 tank showing the cast hull and turret and the long barrelled 90mm M3 gun with its double baffle muzzle brake. Pershings were produced by the Chrysler operated Detroit tank plant who built 246 between March and May 1945, while the Fisher Body Division of General Motors Corporation's Grand Blanc tank arsenal built 1,190 between November 1944 and June 1945. Postwar, the M26, and its improved version, the M46, saw combat with UN forces on South Korea.

The story of the M26 begins in 1942 when the Ordnance Department received the approval of the Services of Supply for its proposed development of the T20 medium tank. This tank was intended to be an improvement on the M4 series, but Ordnance hoped to be able to use the vehicle for comparative tests of armaments, transmissions and suspensions. Thirteen different models of the T20, T22 and T23 medium tanks were developed and these variously tried different weapons — for example the 76mm gun; different transmissions — for example the 'gas-electric' transmission, also used in the M6 heavy ▶

Above: M26 Pershing heavy tank from the rear. Twenty T26E3 prototypes were sent to Europe as the Zebra Mission early in 1945 and were used by the 3rd and 9th Armored Divisions. The T26E3 was standardised as the M26 Pershing heavy tank early in 1945 and production continued post-war. In May 1946 the M26 was re-classified as the M46 medium tank.

tank; and different suspensions — for example the early form of horizontal volute spring suspension of the Sherman. Development of two heavy tanks followed and these were designated T25 and T26. Both mounted the new T7 90mm gun and used the Ford GAF engine with electric transmissions.

The T26 was given a higher priority, and in the T26E1 the Ford GAF engine drove the vehicle through a hydraulic torque converter in series with planetary reduction gearing. This transmission gave three forward ratios and one reverse and was known as the 'torquematic' transmission. Torsion-bar suspension with a 24in (61cm) track was fitted. The turret was cast, while the hull was fabricated from a combination of castings and rolled plate.

At this point the feelings of the various interested parties began to emerge, and opinions differed widely. Early in 1943 the Armored Command had expressed the view that the war would be won or lost with the M4 medium tank, and as a result of this Ordnance embarked on several improvements to crew safety, mechanical reliability and combat efficiency in the Sherman. The Armored Command also objected to heavy tanks in general on the grounds of weight and size. Army Ground Forces, however, wanted 1,000 of the T26 and 7,000 of the lighter T25, the T26 to be armed with the 76mm gun and the T25 with the 75mm gun. On the other hand the Armored Command wanted neither the T25 nor the T26 but did require the 90mm gun. The T26E2 mounted the 105mm howitzer in a mount which was interchangeable with the 90mm mount, and in the T26E3 Ordnance believed that the best compromise had been reached.

Army Ground Forces preferred to delay any standardisation action until the Armored Board had indicated its satisfaction and approved the vehicle's battleworthiness, so the Secretary of War provided the necessary impetus by

Below: During the 1945 advance into Germany, one Pershing destroyed a Tiger and two PzKpfw Mk IV tanks in a single action. The current US Main Battle Tank, the M60 series, is a direct descendent of the M26 via the M46, M47 and M48 tanks.

sending 20 tanks to the European Theatre of Operations. This 'Zebra Mission' proved the battleworthiness of the T26E3 in the hands of the 3rd and 9th Armored Divisions and standardisation and production then proceeded. It is interesting to note that in June 1944, the European Theatre had reported to Washington that there was no requirement for either the 75mm or 76mm guns but that a mix of 90mm guns and 105mm howitzers in the ratio 1:3 was preferable. This was consistent with the perceived role of the tank in 1944 but conflicts with today's concept of the tank primarily as an anti-tank weapon. The T26E3 was adopted as standard in January 1945 under the designation M26 Heavy Tank, and the name 'Pershing' was given, after General John J. Pershing. At the same time the T26E2 with the 105mm howitzer was adopted as the M45 for the close-support role.

The Pershing, although introduced as a heavy tank, was soon reclassified as a medium tank and production continued well past the end of World War II. Although too late to make any real contribution to that war, the M26 was widely used in the Korean War and later supplied to many armies in the Free World.

As was usually the case, the Pershing led to a family of specialist vehicles. The 'Heavyweight Combat Team' was intended to consist of the T84 8in Howitzer Motor Carriage, the T92 240mm Howitzer Motor Carriage, the T93 8in Gun Motor Carriage, the T31 Cargo Carrier and the T12 Recovery Vehicle. A flamethrower tank, cargo tractor and combat engineer vehicle were also produced and consideration was also given to a mine resistant vehicle, based on the M26 chassis, to breach anti-tank minefields. Improvements to the engine and gun resulted in the M46 Medium Tank, the first 'Patton', although the poor turret and cupola shape were retained. From the T26 series, further heavy tanks resulted under the designations T29, T30, T32 and T34. The T30 was equipped with a 155mm gun which fired semi-fixed ammunition, but development was dropped when it became apparent that such a vehicle would not be sufficiently effective relative to its weight. The same fate befell the T29, T32 and T34 for similar reasons.

OTHER NATIONS

While France, Germany, Great Britain, the Soviet Union and the United States are well known for their tank building activities during World War II, it is often not realised that other countries such as Australia, Canada, Czechoslovakia, Italy, Japan and Poland also built tanks in this period. For example, Canada built some 1,420 Valentine tanks between 1941 and 1943 and most of these were sent to Russia. Canada also designed the Ram I and II cruiser tanks; these were not used in combat but were invaluable for training. The chassis of the Ram was also used as a command and observation post vehicle, recovery vehicle and an APC.

Italy, short of funds as usual, concentrated its efforts on tankettes and light tanks which were well suited to combat against lightly armed troops in the colonies but proved fatal to their crews when used in the North African campaigns from 1940 onwards. The standard medium tank of the Italian Army was the Carro Armato M 13/39 which entered service in 1939 but was soon phased out of production in favour of the M 13/40 which had a 47mm instead of 37mm gun. This was followed by the M 14/41 (1,103 built) and the M 15/42 (less than 100 built), but this design was obsolete as soon as it entered production. In 1943 the long-awaited P40, armed with a 75mm gun, entered production but none had entered service by the time the

Italian Army surrendered to the Allies on 8 September 1943.

Japan took an interest in tanks in the early 1920s and by the late 1930s had developed a fairly complete range of tanks to meet its own specific requirements. The majority of these were powered by diesel engine instead of the more common petrol engine; not only did this give them increased operational range but also reduced the chances of fire. In most of the Japanese campaigns, the lightly armed and armoured Japanese tanks were sufficient, as their main role was that of supporting infantry since the Allies had few tanks deployed in the Far East at this time. Once the Japanese advance had been halted, the Allies started to use tanks in the infantry support role. In Burma the British used Grants, while in the island campaigns the Americans used Shermans and these proved capable of easily defeating the Japanese tanks, which in any case were normally used in the static defence role. There were few tank-versus-tank battles in the Philippines towards the end of the war.

In addition to tanks, Japan did develop a number of self-propelled guns and some interesting amphibious tanks. These were originally developed for the Army but development was subsequently taken over by the Navy since they were to be used by the Japanese Marines. Some of these vehicles carried a naval torpedoe on the hull sides.

Ram I and II Cruiser Tanks

Country of origin: Canada.
Crew: 5.
Armament: One 2pounder gun; one .3in machine-gun co-axial with main armament; one .3in machine-gun in cupola on hull top; one .3in machine-gun for anti-aircraft use.
Armour: 90mm (3.56in) maximum.
Dimensions: Length 19ft (5.791m); width 9ft 5in (2.87m); height 8ft 9in (2.667m).
Weight: Combat 64,000lbs (29,030kg).
Ground pressure: 13.3lb/in² (0.94kg/cm²).
Engine: Continental R975-EC2 nine-cylinder radial developing 400bhp at 2,400rpm.
Performance: Road speed 25mph (40.2km/h); road range 144 miles (232km); vertical obstacle 2ft (0.609m); trench 7ft 5in (2.26m); gradient 60 per cent.
History: Used only for training.

In 1940 the Canadian armoured forces consisted of two Vickers tanks, 12 Carden-Loyd carriers and 14 new Mk VI light tanks. Further tanks were not available as Britain did not have enough tanks to meet even her own requirements. The Canadians were able to purchase 219 American M1917 two-man tanks and a few Mk VIII tanks from the United States as scrap. These fulfilled a valuable training role until further and more modern tanks were available. Canada's first venture into tank construction was to build the British Valentine tank, 1,420 being built between 1941 and 1943. Of

Below: The RAM I tank was designed and built by the Montreal Locomotive Works in 1941 and was based on M3 Grant chassis.

these 30 were kept in Canada for training and the remaining 1,390 were supplied to the Russians. Manufacture of the Valentine was undertaken at the Canadian Pacific Railway workshops at Angus, Montreal, and was a result of a British rather than a Canadian order.

In 1940 the Canadians started looking for a cruiser tank to meet the requirements of the Canadian Armoured Corps, and finally decided to take the chassis of the American M3 Grant tank and redesign the hull to accept a turret with a traverse of 360°, rather than have a gun mounted in the side of the hull with limited traverse. The first prototype was completed by the Montreal Locomotive Works in June 1941, production starting late in 1941. The first vehicles were known as the Ram I, but only 50 of these were built before production switched to the Ram II, which had a 6pounder gun. Some 1,899 Ram IIs had been built by the time production was completed in July 1943.

The Ram I had a hull of all-cast construction. The driver was seated at the front of the hull on the right with the small machine-gun turret to his left. This latter was armed with a .3in machine-gun and had a traverse of 120° left and 50° right. The other three crew members were in the turret in the centre of the hull, the turret being a casting with the front part bolted into position. The main armament consisted of a 2pounder gun with an elevation of +20° and a depression of −10° and a .3in M1919A4 machine-gun was mounted co-axially with the main armament. A similar weapon could be mounted on the commander's cupola for use in the anti-aircraft role. Some 171 rounds of 2pounder and 4,275 rounds of .3in machine-gun ammunition were carried.

The Ram II was armed with a 6pounder gun, and the small turret on the hull was replaced by a more conventional ball-type mounting. A total of 92 rounds of 6pounder and 4,000 rounds of .3in machine-gun ammunition was carried. Other modifications of the Ram II over the earlier vehicle included the elimination of the side doors in the hull, a modified suspension, a modified clutch, new air cleaners and so on. Most Rams were shipped to ▶

Britain where they were used by the 4th and 5th Canadian Armoured Divisions, although these formations were re-equipped with Shermans before the invasion of Europe in June 1944, so the Ram did not see combat.

There were a number of variants of the Ram tank, and some of these did see combat. The Ram Command and Observation Post Vehicle had a crew of six, and in appearance was almost identical to the normal tank, although it had only a dummy gun and the turret could be traversed through a mere 90° by hand wheel. Internally, additional communication equipment was provided. Eighty-four Ram COPVs were built. A Ram Armoured Vehicle Royal Engineers was developed, but this did not enter service. The Ram was also used as an ammunition carrier and as a towing vehicle for the 17 pounder anti-tank gun. Perhaps the most famous version of the vehicle was the Ram Kangaroo. In 1944 the Canadian II Corps had to carry out an assault in Falaise in Normandy, and as there were not sufficient half-tracks available,

Above: The Ram II was armed with a 6pounder in place of the 2pounder of the Ram I. Neither version was ever used in combat.

they used as APCs some American M7 105mm Priest SPGs with their guns removed. Later it was decided to do the same with the Rams, as there were plenty of these in England. By the end of 1944 special battalions, equipped with Kangaroos, had been formed by both the British and Canadians. The conversion of the Ram was simple, and carried out at REME workshops. Basically, the turret was removed and benches were provided for 10 to 12 troops. The Kangaroo remained in service with the British and Canadian Armies for some years after the war. There was also a Ram Armoured Recovery Vehicle. Finally there was the Ram flamethrower, known as the Badger, which was used operationally in Holland early in 1945. The flame-gun was mounted in place of the bow machine-gun.

Carro Armato M 13/40 Medium Tank

M 13/40, M 14/41, M 15/42, P40 (P26), and Semovente M42M, M42T.
Country of origin: Italy.
Crew: 4.
Armament: One 47mm gun; one 8mm machine-gun co-axial with main armament; one 8mm anti-aircraft machine-gun; twin 8mm machine-guns in hull front.
Armour: 42mm (1.65in) maximum; 6mm (0.24in) minimum.
Dimensions: Length 16ft 2in (4.92m); width 7ft 3in (2.2m); height 7ft 10in (2.38m).
Weight: Combat 30,865lbs (14,000kg).
Ground Pressure: 13.2lb/in² (0.92kg/cm²).
Engine: SPA 8 TM40 eight-cylinder diesel developing 125hp.
Performance: Road speed 20mph (32km/h); road range 125 miles (200km); vertical obstacle 2ft 8in (0.8m); trench 6ft 11in (2.1m); gradient 70 per cent.
History: Entered service with Italian Army in 1940 and phased out of service in 1942.

The Carro Armato M 11/39 was designed in 1936 with the first prototype being completed the following year. This used some suspension components of the L3 tankette. Armament consisted of twin turret-mounted Breda 8mm machine-guns and a 37mm gun mounted in the right side of the hull. The 37mm gun could be traversed through 30° and had an elevation of +12° and

Below: A Carro Armato M 13/40 medium tank (No. 1, 3 Ptn, 2 Coy, XI Bn) now preserved as a memorial to Italians killed at El Alamein. The tank was armed with an effective high-velocity 47mm gun but its thin armour made it vulnerable to many anti-tank weapons on the battlefield. At least two Allied units, the British 6th Royal Tank Regiment and the Australian 6th Cavalry, were equipped with captured M 13/40s in 1941.

a depression of −8°, and 84 rounds of 37mm and 2,808 rounds of 8mm ammunition were carried.

The M 11/39, of which only 100 were built, weighed 10.83 tons (11,000kg) and had a crew of three, and saw action in North Africa in 1940–41. It soon became apparent that the main armament would have to be mounted in a turret rather than in the hull front with a limited traverse. The chassis of the M 11/39 was retained, but the hull was redesigned, to form the first prototype of the M 13/40, completed in 1940, with first production tanks being completed in the same year. Main armament consisted of a turret-mounted 47mm gun with an elevation of +20° and a depression of −10°. An 8mm machine-gun was mounted co-axial with the main armament and there was a similar weapon for the anti-aircraft role. Two 8mm machine-guns were mounted in the hull front on the right. Some 104 rounds of 47mm and 3,048 rounds of 8mm ammunition were carried. The hull was of bolted construction with a minimum thickness of 0.24in (6mm) and a maximum thickness of 1.65in (42mm). The driver and bow machine-gunner were seated in the front of the hull, and the loader and commander in the turret. The commander had to aim and fire the main armament in addition to his other duties. The suspension on each side consisted of four double-wheeled articulated bogies, mounted in two assemblies, each of the latter being carried on semi-elliptic springs. The drive sprocket was at the front and the idler at the rear, and there were three track-return rollers.

The M 13/40 was used in North Africa in 1941 and was found to be very prone to breakdowns as it was not designed to operate in desert conditions. The M 13/40 was followed in production by the M 14/41 which had a more powerful engine developing 145hp and fitted with filters to allow it to operate in the desert. The last model in the series was the M 15/42, which entered service in 1943. This had a slightly longer hull than the earlier models ▶

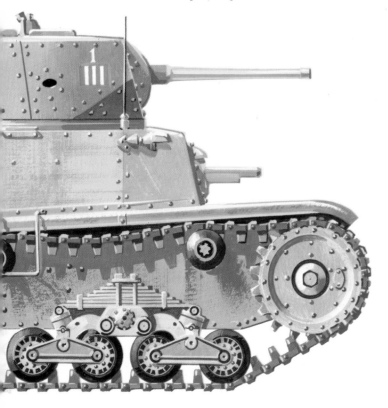

Above: US Army personnel inspect a captured M 13/40 tank. The type saw service in North Africa, Greece and Yugoslavia. The chassis was also used for a number of self-propelled guns.

and was powered by an eight-cylinder petrol engine which developed 192hp, this giving the tank a top road speed of 25mph (40km/h). Other modifications included the re-siting of the hull escape door on the right of the hull, a longer gun barrel, power-operated turret traverse and heavier armour.

Production of the tanks was undertaken by Ansaldo-Fossati and the following quantities were built: M 13/40 799, M 14/41 1,103 and M 15/42 between 82 and 90. The M 13/40 and M 14/41 were the most important Italian tanks of World War II and were used in North Africa, Greece and Yugoslavia. Many were captured when they ran out of fuel and at least two Allied units, the British 6th Royal Tank Regiment and the Australian 6th Cavalry, were equipped with these tanks for a brief time when British tanks were in short supply in 1941.

The Italians developed a variety of self-propelled artillery based on these chassis. The *Semovente* M40, M41 and M42 were based respectively on the M13, M14 and M15 chassis. Armament consisted of a Model 35 75mm gun/ howitzer with an elevation of +22° and a depression of −12°, traverse being 20° left and 18° right. There was also a command model with the main

armament removed. This was armed with a hull-mounted 13.2mm machine-gun and an 8mm anti-aircraft machine-gun. The *Semovente* M42M (75/14) self-propelled gun was to have been based on the P40 tank chassis but as a result of delays less than 100 were built, and these were based on the M 15/42 chassis. Armament consisted of a 75mm gun with 42 rounds of ammunition. This was followed by the M42L which had a 105mm gun. When the Germans took over the Ansaldo works they built a model known as the M42T which had a 75mm gun.

The M 13/40, M 14/41 and M 15/42 were to have been replaced by a new tank designated the P40 (or P26). Although design work on this tank started as early as 1940, it was not until 1942 that the first prototype was ready for trials. The delays were caused by changes in the main armament and the difficulty in finding a suitable engine for the tank. The tank entered production in 1943 but did not enter service with the Italian Army, although a few appear to have been used in the static defence role by the Germans in Italy. The P40 weighed 25.59 tons (26,000kg) and was armed with a 75mm gun and an 8mm co-axial machine-gun. The P40 was itself to have been followed by the P43, but this latter only reached the mock-up stage. The Italians also designed a tank called the *Carro Armato Celere Sahariano*, which had a Christie suspension and resembled the Crusader which the Italians encountered in North Africa, but this never entered production.

Type 95 HA-GO Light Tank

Country of origin: Japan.
Crew: 3.
Armament: One Type 94 37mm gun; Type 91 6.5mm machine-gun in hull front (see text).
Armour: 12mm (0.47in) maximum; 6mm (0.25in) minimum.
Dimensions: Length 14ft 4in (4.38m); width 6ft 9in (2.057m); height 7ft 2in (2.184m).
Weight: Combat 16,314lbs (7,400kg).
Ground Pressure: 8.7lb/in² (0.61kg/cm²).
Engine: Mitsubishi Model NVD 6120 six-cylinder air-cooled diesel developing 120hp at 1,800rpm.
Performance: Road speed 28mph (45km/h); range 156 miles (250km); vertical obstacle 2ft 8in (0.812m); trench 6ft 7in (2m); gradient 60 per cent.
History: Entered service with Japanese Army in 1935 and remained in service until 1945.

In 1934 Mitsubishi Heavy Industries built the prototype of a new light tank, which was tested in both China and Japan, and followed by a second prototype the following year. This was standardised as the Type 95 light tank but was also known as the *HA-GO* (this being the Mitsubishi name) or the *KE-GO* (this being its official Japanese Army name). Although most sources state that Mitsubishi built the prototype, others claim that these were built at the Sagami Arsenal.

The Type 95 was used by the cavalry and the infantry, and saw action in both China and throughout the World War II (or the Great East Asia War as the Japanese call it). Production amounted to about 1,250 tanks, most of which were built by Mitsubishi although numerous other companies and arsenals were also involved in component manufacture. When it was originally built the Type 95 compared well with other light tanks of that period, but by the early part of World War II it had become outdated, as indeed had most Japanese armoured vehicles. The Japanese used the Type 95 in small units or wasted them in the static defence role in many of the islands that they overran in the Pacific area.

The hull of the tank was of riveted and welded construction varying in thickness from 0.35in (9mm) to 0.55in (14mm). The driver was seated at the front of the hull on the right, with the bow machine-gunner to his left. The

commander, who also had to load, aim and fire the gun, was seated in the turret, which was offset to the left of the hull. The engine and transmission were at the rear of the hull, and the crew could reach the engine from within the hull. The inside of the tank was provided with a layer of asbestos padding in an effort to keep the temperature as low as possible, and this also gave the crew some protection against personal injury when the tank was travelling across very rough country. There was a space between the asbestos and the hull to allow air to circulate. The suspension was of the well-tried bellcrank type and consisted of four road wheels (two per bogie), with the drive sprocket at the front and the idler at the rear. There were two track-return rollers. Some of the Type 95s used in Manchuria had their suspensions modified as it was found that severe pitching occurred when the tank was crossing the local terrain, and these were redesignated the Type 35 (Special).

Armament consisted of a turret-mounted 37mm tank gun which could fire both HE and AP rounds, and a Type 61 6.5mm machine-gun mounted ▶

Right and below: Front, rear and top views of Type 95 HA-GO light tank. This entered service with the Japanese Army in 1935 and remained in service until 1945, although by this time it was hopelessly out of date by any standard. One of the many disadvantages of the tank was that the commander had to load, aim and fire the 37mm gun. Some 1,250 HA-GO tanks were built.

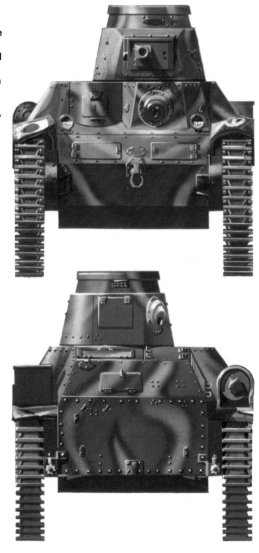

in the front of the hull with a traverse of 35° left and right. Later the Type 61 gun was replaced by a Type 97 7.7mm machine-gun and a similar weapon was mounted in the turret in the 5 o'clock position, this being operated by the commander/gunner. Later in the war the 37mm Type 94 tank gun was replaced by a Type 98 tank gun, which had a higher muzzle velocity. Some 119 rounds of 37mm and 2,970 rounds of machine-gun ammunition were carried. A number of tanks were also fitted with smoke dischargers on the sides of the hull, towards the rear.

There were a number of variants of the Type 95 light tank, including an amphibious version. In 1943 some Type 95s had their 37mm guns replaced by a 57mm gun as fitted to the Type 97 medium tank, and these vehicles then became the Type 3 light tank. The Type 3 was followed by the Type 4 light tank in 1944: this was a Type 95 with the standard turret removed and replaced by the complete Type 97 medium tank turret with its 47mm gun. The Type 95 was to have been replaced by the Type 98 light tank, and prototypes of this were completed as early as 1938 by both Hino Motors and Mitsubishi Heavy Industries. This did not enter production until 1942, and only 100 seem to have been built (some sources state that 200 were built) before production was stopped in 1943. This model had a more powerful engine, which gave it a higher road speed, and thicker armour. Its suspension consisted of six road wheels with the drive sprocket at the front and the idler at the rear, there being three return rollers. The driver was seated at the front of the hull in the centre. Armament consisted of a 37mm Type 100 tank gun and two Type 97 7.7mm machine-guns.

Other light tanks developed by Japan included the Improved Model 98 which had four road wheels, idler at the front and drive sprocket at the rear. No return rollers were fitted as the top of the track rested on the road wheels. Finally, there were the Type 2 (less than 30 built) and the Type 5, only one of which was built by Hino Motors before the end of the war.

Below: Type 95 HA-GO tank in typical operating environment. The inside of the tank was provided with a layer of asbestos padding in an effort to keep the temperature as low as possible, as well as giving the crew some protection against personal injury when the tank was crossing very rough country. Air was allowed to circulate between this and the hull.

Above: A column of Type 95 HA-GO light tanks with their main and secondary armament removed. These were probably being used for carrying ammunition or other supplies.

Below: A column of Type 95 light tanks moves forward during the Japanese invasion of Luzon in the Philippines in 1941/42.

Type 97 CHI-HA Medium Tank

Country of origin: Japan.
Crew: 4.
Armament: One Type 90 57mm gun; one 7.7mm Type 97 machine-gun in turret rear; one 7.7mm Type 97 machine-gun in bow.
Armour: 25mm (0.98in) maximum; 8mm (0.3in) minimum.
Dimensions: Length 18ft 1in (5.516m); width 7ft 8in (2.33m); height 7ft 4in (2.23m).
Weight: Combat 33,069lbs (15,000kg).
Engine: Mitsubishi 12-cylinder air-cooled diesel developing 170hp at 2,000rpm.
Performance: Road speed 24mph (38km/h); range 130 miles (210km); vertical obstacle 2ft 6in (0.812m); trench 8ft 3in (2.514m); gradient 57 per cent.
History: Entered service with the Japanese Army in 1938 and continued in service until 1945. Also used by China after World War II.

The standard Japanese medium tank in the 1930s was the Type 89, but by 1936 it had become apparent that this would have to be replaced by a more modern vehicle. The General Staff Office and the Engineering Department could not agree on the best design, so two different prototypes were built. Osaka Arsenal built a prototype to the design of the General Staff, called the *CHI-NI*, whilst Mitsubishi built the model of the Engineering Department, called the *CHI-HA*.

The *CHI-NI* weighed just under 9.84 tons (10,000kg) and was powered by a six-cylinder air-cooled diesel developing 135hp, which gave the tank a top speed of 18.5mph (30km/h). The *CHI-NI* had a three-man crew, and was armed with a 57mm Type 90 tank gun and a 6.5mm Type 91 machine-gun.

The Mitsubishi design was much heavier and weighed 15 tons (15,241kg). It was powered by a Mitsubishi 12-cylinder air-cooled diesel which developed 170hp and gave the tank a top road speed of 24mph (38km/h). Armament consisted of a 57mm gun and two 7.7mm machine-guns. The *CHI-HA* had a crew of four, of whom two were in the turret. Both of these prototypes were completed in 1937 and were subjected to comparative trials. Both tanks had good and bad points, however, and it was not until war broke out in China that it was decided to place the Mitsubishi tank in production as the Type 97 (*CHI-HA*) medium tank. Even today, many feel that the *CHI-NI* could have been developed into a first-class light tank.

Most Type 97s were built by Mitsubishi, although other companies, including Hitachi, also built the tank. The hull was of riveted and welded construction. The driver was seated at the front of the hull on the right, with the bow machine-gunner to his left. The two-man turret was in the centre of the hull and offset to the right. The engine was at the rear of the hull, and power was transmitted to the gearbox in the front of the hull by a propeller-shaft which ran down the centreline of the hull. The suspension consisted of six dual rubber-tired road wheels, with the drive sprocket at the front and the idler at the rear. There were three track-return rollers, although the centre one ▶

Left and below: Front and rear views of the Type 97 medium tank clearly showing the turret offset to the right of the hull and the 7.7mm Type 97 machine gun in the rear of the turret. Main armament was a 57mm Type 90 gun with another 7.7mm Type 97 machine gun in the bow to left of the driver's position.

Left: A Type 97 tank of 3rd Company, 7th Tank Regiment, advances through the jungle on the Bataan peninsula during the invasion of the Philippines in 1942. Note the smoke dischargers above the 57mm gun and the radio frame aerial circumscribing the turret which was a characteristic feature of Japanese tanks.

supported the inside of the track only. The four central bogie wheels were paired and mounted on bellcranks resisted by armoured compression springs. Each end road wheel was independently bellcrank-mounted to the hull in a similar fashion.

Armament consisted of a short-barrelled 57mm Model 97 tank gun, firing HE and AP rounds, a 7.7mm Model 97 machine-gun in the rear of the turret and a machine-gun of the same type in the bow of the tank. The main armament had an elevation of +11° and a depression of −9°, turret traverse being 360°. Two sets of trunnions allowed the gun to be traversed independently of the turret. The inner vertical trunnions, set in a heavy steel bracket fitted to the cradle, permitted a 5° left and right traverse. Some 120 rounds (80 HE and 40 AP) of 57mm and 2,350 rounds of machine-gun ammunition were carried. The large provision of HE ammunition compared to other tanks of this period was because the Japanese believed that the role of the tank was to support the infantry rather than to destroy enemy armour.

Compared with those of earlier Japanese tanks, the turret of the Type 97 was a great improvement: at last the tank commander could command the tank rather than operate the main armament. In later years, the large-diameter turret-ring fitted enabled the tank to be up-armed as more powerful weapons became available. As a result of combat experience gained against Soviet forces during the Nomonhan incident of 1939, it was decided that a gun with a higher muzzle velocity was required. A new turret was designed by Mitsubishi and when installed on the Type 97 it raised the tank's weight to 15.75 tons (16,000kg). These tanks were known as the Type 97 (Special). The gun fitted was the 47mm Type 1 (1941), which had a long barrel by Japanese standards and could fire both HE and AP rounds. The latter had a muzzle velocity of 2,700fps (823m/s) and would penetrate 2.76in (70mm) of armour at a range of 500 yards (457m). The breech-block was of the semi-automatic vertical sliding type. Some 104 rounds of 47mm and 2,575 rounds of machine-gun ammunition were carried.

There were many variants of the Type 97 medium tank: flail type mine-clearing tank, bulldozer tank, a variety of self-propelled guns, an anti-aircraft tank with a 20mm gun, bridge laying tank and a number of different engineer and recovery models, to name a few. One of the most unusual models was the ram tank (*HO-K*), which had its turret removed and a steel prow mounted

Above left: Japanese Type 97 tanks drive down a road at Bukit Timah, Singapore. The main role of these was infantry support.

Above: Type 97 CHI-HA medium tanks in Singapore. One of the major improvements of this tank over earlier Japanese tanks was the provision of a two-man turret which enabled the commander to command the tank rather than operating the main armament.

at the front of the hull, developed for clearing a path through forests in Manchuria.

The Type 97 medium tank was followed by the Type 1 medium tank, or *CHI-NE*. This weighed 17.2 tons (17,476kg) and its armour was increased to a maximum of 2in (50mm). It was powered by a Mitsubishi Type 100 12-cylinder air-cooled diesel which developed 240hp at 2,000rpm. Armament consisted of a Type 1 47mm gun and two Type 97 7.7mm machine-guns, one in the turret rear and one in the hull front. This was followed by the Type 3 (*CHI-NU*) medium tank in 1943. This had the same hull as the Type 1, but a new turret was fitted, increasing weight to 18.8 tons (19,100kg), which reduced top speed to 24mph (38km/h). Armament consisted of a 75mm Type 3 tank gun with a 7.7mm machine-gun in the hull front, there being no machine-gun in the turret rear. Production of the Type 3 commenced in 1944 but only some 50 or 60 examples were built. The Type 4 (*CHI-TO*) had a longer chassis and weighed 30 tons (30,480kg). This was armed with a turret-mounted 75mm gun and a bow-mounted 7.7mm machine-gun, and only a few of these were built.

The final Japanese medium tank was the Type 5 (*CHI-RI*). This weighed 37 tons (37,594kg) and was armed with a turret-mounted 75mm gun and a bow-mounted 37mm gun. Its armour had a maximum thickness of 3in (75mm) and it was powered by a BMW aircraft engine developing 550hp at 1,500rpm. This gave the tank a top road speed of 28mph (45km/h). The suspension consisted of eight road wheels with the drive sprocket at the front and the idler at the rear, and there were three track-return rollers. This tank did not reach the production stage, however. If it had, it would have been a difficult tank for the Americans to destroy, although by the end of the war, the superior M26 Pershing had been deployed to the Pacific area.

GUIDES IN THIS SERIES...........

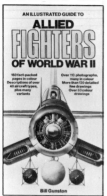

AN ILLUSTRATED GUIDE TO

ALLIED FIGHTERS
OF WORLD WAR II

160 fact-packed
pages in colour
Descriptions of over
40 aircraft types,
plus many
variants

Over 110 photographs,
many in colour
More than 120 detailed
line drawings
Over 60 colour
drawings

Bill Gunston

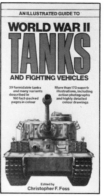

AN ILLUSTRATED GUIDE TO

WORLD WAR II TANKS
AND FIGHTING VEHICLES

39 formidable tanks
and many variants
described in
160 fact-packed
pages in colour

More than 170 superb
illustrations, including
action photographs
and highly detailed
colour drawings

Edited by
Christopher F. Foss

AN ILLUSTRATED GUIDE TO

RIFLES
AND SUB-MACHINE GUNS

43 modern rifles and 35 sub-machine guns
All photographed in full colour
35,000 words of text

Major Frederick Myatt M.C.

AN ILLUSTRATED GUIDE TO

GERMAN, ITALIAN AND JAPANESE
FIGHTERS
OF WORLD WAR II
Major Fighters and Attack Aircraft of the Axis Powers

160 fact-packed
pages in colour
Descriptions of over
50 aircraft types,
plus many variants

120 dramatic photographs,
many in colour
More than 180 detailed
line drawings
Over 50 colour drawings

Bill Gunston

AN ILLUSTRATED GUIDE TO

BOMBERS
OF WORLD WAR II

160 fact-packed
pages in colour
Descriptions of well over
50 aircraft types,
plus many variants

More than 160
detailed line drawings
90 dramatic photographs,
many in colour
Over 40 colour drawings

Bill Gunston

AN ILLUSTRATED GUIDE TO

MODERN FIGHTERS
AND ATTACK AIRCRAFT

Fact-packed
descriptions
most in full colour
of 60 of the world's
most exciting
warplanes

120 action photographs
most in full colour
180 line drawings
34 superb
colour profiles

Bill Gunston

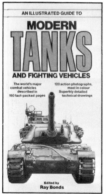

AN ILLUSTRATED GUIDE TO

MODERN TANKS
AND FIGHTING VEHICLES

The world's major
combat vehicles
described in
160 fact-packed pages

120 action photographs,
most in colour
Superbly detailed
technical drawings

Edited by
Ray Bonds

AN ILLUSTRATED GUIDE TO

MODERN WARSHIPS
Over 60 of the world's most exciting warships

160 fact-packed
pages in colour

130 action photographs
Over 60 technical
drawings

Hugh Lyon

* Each has 160 fact-filled pages
* Each is colourfully illustrated with more than one hundred
  dramatic photographs, and often with superb technical drawings
* Each contains concisely presented data and accurate descriptions
  of major international weapons
* Each represents tremendous value

Further titles in this series are in preparation
Your military library will be incomplete without them